Practicing Intercultural Communication

Ellen Shide Crannell

West Valley College

KENDALL/HUNT PUBLISHING COMPANY
4050 Westmark Drive   Dubuque, Iowa 52002

Thank you to Monica Flores-Mason for your significant contribution and encouragement in the preparation of this book. It could not have been done without you. Thank you, also, to Sheila Shadrick, who spent many hours tediously transcribing and editing. Of course, this book could not have been completed without the vital contributions of incidents and activities submitted by colleagues and students. To Piper McNulty, Marcy Betlach, and colleagues and students at West Valley College, Mission College, De Anza College, and San Jose State University, thank you for your innovative ideas, advice, and support. All your efforts are very truly appreciated.

Contents

Preface

While studying and then teaching intercultural communication, I found the use of critical incidents to be most enlightening. However, many of the critical incident resources at my disposal were of international focus, mainly dealing with international businesspeople or wealthy travelers. Consequently, I found myself using incidents that my students couldn't really relate to their own lives. Conversely, I also found that students were much more motivated to discuss incidents that happened in their own lives. Hence, I began my collection of critical incidents written by my own students at various colleges in the Bay Area. Diversity surrounds us, so why not focus on intercultural issues at home instead of searching for them overseas?

This book has become a collaboration of students' stories and colleagues' classroom activities in the hopes that it will be a useful resource as a supplemental text in the intercultural communication classroom. It is my hope that this volume will grow over the years as more intercultural communication scholars make contributions, assuring a variety of intercultural activities, discussions, stories, and resources. If you'd like to make a contribution to this collection please send a hard copy and the permissions form found in the appendix.

Please send contributions for future editions to:

Ellen Shide Crannell
Communication Studies
West Valley College
14000 Fruitvale Avenue
Saratoga, CA 95070

Each chapter begins with critical incidents. These are wonderful self-quizzes for the intercultural communication student and provide opportunity for discussion in the classroom. The "comments" section of each chapter highlights some of the salient issues introduced in the incidents. At the end of the chapter are a variety of classroom activities and discussion questions. Students can work directly through the chapters, or instructors can assign portions when relevant. No matter how the book is utilized, it will provide marvelous opportunities to explore intercultural concepts in a very real way. I hope you have as much fun reading through the selections as I did.

Introduction

This book provides you with resources to help you understand the intercultural communication concepts you are learning about in class. Your instructor may require you to read through the entire selection or may select particular sections that apply to a specific class objective. Each selection is designed to help you understand the practical applications of a particular concept. In other words, the selection should help you to understand how intercultural communication concepts work in real life.

The critical incidents are short stories, written by intercultural communication students, that illustrate the communication problems that occur when interacting interculturally. They are designed to serve as self-quizzes. As you read each incident, decide which option you think best answers the dilemma presented and circle the correct answer. Doing this before reading the "Analysis of Options" section will allow you to test your intercultural knowledge. The "Analysis of Options" section will then tell you which answer is correct.

Additional information can be found in the "Comments" section of each chapter. This section will elaborate on the intercultural communication concepts illustrated in each incident. Therefore, it will not only help you to understand the concepts but also explain the incidents further and connect them together.

Finally, each chapter has an "Exercises" section. This section includes activities to be done in and out of class. Furthermore, the "Personal Assessment Questions" give you an opportunity to reflect on your own experiences with the concepts presented in the chapter. All "Exercises" are tools to stimulate classroom discussion, so make note of your answers in the book so that you are prepared to discuss them in class.

My intercultural communication students and colleagues have had a lot of fun sharing these stories and utilizing the activities. If you use them to help you celebrate culture, you will find it a rewarding experience.

Chapter One _____

_____ Language ___

1

As a local elementary school secretary, it was part of my job to greet the public and register new students. As in most schools in the Silicon Valley, my school had a very diverse population. One fall morning, I found myself greeting a Korean family: the mother, grandmother, a young child, and two toddlers. They were very pleasant and very patient and very eager to have their young child start school. I explained the various forms. I asked them several questions such as, "Does your child speak any English? Has your child had her immunizations? Did your child attend school anywhere else?" To every question, the mother and grandmother would smile and say, "yes." The mother filled out the papers and showed me her child's passport. Based on her answers and the information on the forms, I placed the child in first grade. The child was born in December and could have been placed in either kindergarten or first grade. The following afternoon, the teacher approached me with concerns about the child's immaturity and felt she belonged in kindergarten. After the Principal conferenced with the mother, she discovered that the child had never attended school before. I had made a mistake. I realized that the mother had answered yes to my question regarding previous schooling. Was she trying to skip her child up a grade? Did she not understand the questions?

What could I do to make sure that I did not repeat my error?

Options

1. Always have an interpreter.
2. Ask open-ended questions that require specific information, not just yes or no answers.
3. Inform new families that I need accurate information for the registration process.
4. Always place children who speak English as a second language in the lower grade.

Analysis of Options

1. This was not always possible especially considering the number of different languages spoken by the students and their families at my school. I could sometimes call on a student in 4th or 5th grade to help me with the registration process, and I quickly learned which students I could call to the office to help me. This may be an effective solution when possible, but it is often not possible.
2. This turned out to be my most effective method. I was better able to ascertain how well people understood what I asked and what I was saying when I used this method. I was told by a teacher that the Koreans did not answer "no" to any of my questions because that is considered a rude response in their culture. So they understood my questions, but answered them in a way that I could not interpret.

3. This does not really solve the problem. Some families would probably still give inaccurate information in order to avoid being rude.
4. This is not a good solution. Assuming a child's ability based on his or her culture is stereotyping and is most often inaccurate. This would only create more problems.

2

It was nearing twilight and my friend and I were on a quest for a heater for his room. We had already visited Target, and he had found it to be too expensive. We decided to check out some thrift stores to see if they might carry a less expensive one. Considering I knew that there was a Good Will located on Saratoga - Sunnyvale Road, this became our destination. Upon entering the store I noticed an elderly white woman leaning against the check out counter looking perturbed and frustrated. Behind the counter a middle aged Chinese woman stood trying to explain what I perceived to be a store policy. Not wanting to interfere my friend and I made our way to the back of the store where the electronic equipment was piled high on shelves. Seeing as I was there, I picked up a few items that I thought might complement my apartment. Unable to find a heater there, my friend was anxious to leave and be on to the next store. As we approached the counter to purchase the items I'd chosen I noticed that the two ladies who were previously at the counter were still engaged in conversation displaying intonations that I saw as frustration. I got behind the white woman and waited to be rung up, giving me a chance to listen in on their conversation. The Chinese woman had very broken English and was trying to explain to the white woman that the Good Will's return policy was not cash, but store credit. The white woman continued to ask whether or not she would be given a return on her money if she were to return an item. It seemed apparent to me that the white woman's understanding of how a return policy could be described was not being said, and therefore she would continue to ask the same question until she could decode what the Chinese woman meant. Her expression was that of confusion and fatigue. The Chinese woman seemed agitated that the white woman did not understand her explanation. Maybe I shouldn't have, but considering that I was going to have to wait until the conversation was resolved, I decided to intervene; after all I did understand what the Chinese woman meant, and I also knew how to convey this to the white woman. I looked at the white woman and said, "I think what she is trying to say is that if you buy an item and return it you will not receive cash back. However the amount that you spent on the item returned will be available for you to use for another purchase at this store." I then looked at the Chinese woman for confirmation. She nodded and began to ring me up. The white woman said, "oh thank you" in a curt tone, and left.

What went wrong?

Options

1. The white woman was glad to understand, but perhaps annoyed that their conversation had taken over ten minutes.
2. She was unhappy with the store's policy.
3. The Chinese woman was at fault because she could not accurately represent the store due to her broken English.
4. The white woman was at fault because she was not attempting to understand the Chinese woman.

Analysis of Options

1. This is the best response. Communicating with someone from another culture is difficult work. It requires more time and energy than communicating with someone who has a similar communication style. The frustration and confusion that accompany the interpretation of a different communication style often result in extreme emotional reactions. Hence, when people communicate interculturally, even successfully, they may leave the situation feeling annoyed, angry, paranoid, depressed, or tense. These emotional reactions tend to decrease as intercultural competence increases.

2. This is unlikely. Once she understood the policy she didn't argue with the clerk.
3. Often when people misunderstand each other they place the blame on the other person. This is detrimental to the communication process. It immediately sets up barriers and fosters ethnocentrism and prejudice. Considering the diversity of the United States, it is futile to expect everyone to communicate in the same way. There is a better answer.
4. Again, placing blame is not to anyone's benefit here. It's impossible to determine if the white woman was attempting to understand the Chinese woman or not. It's difficult to listen for a style of communication you are not expecting, and if one has not studied communication skills it becomes even more of an obstacle. There is a better answer.

3

Four months ago, I went to get my nails done at Tina's Nail Shop. The shop is owned by Koreans with Korean workers. My incident occurred with one of the workers who never did my nails before, so we didn't know each other. We didn't know how to communicate. She knew a little bit of English, but I couldn't understand her. I was frustrated because I felt that she should be able to speak to me since she was in America doing business. And she was frustrated because I wasn't understanding her, so she felt like I was belittling her. When the time came for me to pay her she said fifteen dollars and I thought she said fifty. I said, "Are you sure because that is not the price that Tina charges me?" The lady's tone of voice was in a high pitch when she exclaimed, "YES!" So I got very upset and asked to speak to Tina.

How could you best explain this incident?

Options

1. The Korean worker was rude.
2. I was wrong for expecting the worker to speak English just because she was in the United States.
3. Koreans have different speech patterns than U.S. Americans.

Analysis of Options

1. Before I went to the nail shop I should have been better prepared to communicate with the Korean woman.
2. Instead of the Korean woman telling me the price of my nails she should have had a price list near her to show the price so there would be no confusion between the two of them.
3. The best response would be that the two women should learn how to communicate better with different cultures so that they wouldn't take offense to things that are misunderstood. Different cultures often use the same words but different meanings. They also have different tones. A high pitch to a U.S. American may be rude but to another culture it may not mean that. Also they should not have been so quick to blame each other for the miscommunication problem. This could be resolved by stating your own assumptions so that there would be no mix up.

4

About a month ago, my incident took place where I work. I work at Long's Drugs, and we have all sorts of different customers. This one happened to be Vietnamese. She came up to me and asked "where d- - - - - at?" I had no idea what she was trying to tell me, so I asked her to repeat what she said. This time she added something else to what she wanted. I somewhat understood (at least I thought I did), so I took her to where the item was located. Well, it turned out that this wasn't what she asked for. So she repeated what she had said and started to make hand gestures to describe what she was looking for. This didn't help, so now we were both annoyed with each other because of the language barrier between us. So I try to name things that sound similar to what she said, and she starts to yell at me. Now we are just plain pissed off at each other. She's ranting and raving over whatever the hell it is that she wants and I'm stuck trying to find it. The first thing that comes to my mind is to have her write it down, so I asked her to write it down and she goes ballistic on me. She throws her arms in the air and says something to me (probably cussing me out). So I give her a look saying "yeah, you're not a psychopath!" She makes a fist like she wants to hit me, then turns around and storms down the isle mumbling various profanities (in very understandable English, I might add). Lucky for me she found what she was looking for (vacuum bags) and didn't come back to kill me!!

What could have been done differently?

Options

1. I could have been more understanding.
2. She could learn to speak English.
3. I could have asked a fellow employee to help me.
4. I could have apologized to her for not understanding and expressed my regret at not being able to help.

Analysis of Options

1. Although I felt I did the best I possibly could, this obviously didn't work.
2. While this would be nice, it's not realistic.
3. There is the possibility that my co-worker would have understood what she wanted, but there is also the chance that I could have dragged another unsuspecting person into a situation that they didn't know how to handle.
4. Although the misunderstanding was not necessarily my fault, communication with this woman would have been smoother had she not felt that I was annoyed by her. With English being her second language, she probably felt the same frustration with many other conversations, not just ours. Expressing my regret may have helped her to understand that I was at least trying to understand and that it was not necessarily her fault either.

5

Martha is Filipino and her boyfriend, Robert, is Mexican. Martha's friend invited them to a party so she told her boyfriend that she would pick him up at 5 and that he needed to be "dressed" already. She showed up wearing jeans and a shirt and he was wearing slacks and a nice sweater. He was rather irritated because she told him to get "dressed." He said to her, "You should have said get ready."

Why did they misunderstand each other?

Options

1. Although they both speak English, words or slang can have different meanings to them.
2. She really wanted him to be "dressed up."
3. He just wanted to go to the party "dressed up."
4. Martha wanted Robert to look better than everyone else at the party.

Analysis of Options

1. In the Filipino language, there is only one way of saying "get ready or dress up." In Robert's language, there is a difference between get ready (casual) and dressed up (semi formal). What we have here is simply a difference in *semantics*, referring to what we intend words to mean.
2. Martha probably did not want Robert dressed up if she was not dressed up herself. There is a better answer.
3. Robert's final statements indicate he cared about dressing appropriately. There is a better answer.
4. There is nothing in the story to indicate this. Choose again.

6

When I came to the U.S. I didn't know much about the culture. After a week, my brother took me to "Safeway" to buy some groceries. We finished picking up things from the counters, and he asked me to stand in line so that he could get his check ready. When my turn came, the woman at the checkout counter billed the items and asked me for paper or plastic. I mistook it for a credit card and said that he'll be paying by check. I asked her to put the items in a cover. She never followed it, and she made a rude face at me. She said that this is all she had, and dumped everything into it. Later, my brother came and paid the check. I thought that she was rude to me. She just ignored me and moved onto the next person.

Why was the cashier so rude?

Options

1.   I think she didn't follow my accent.
2.   She might have mistaken my usage of words.
3.   She didn't have the patience to listen to me.
4.   She didn't like the manner in which I answered to her.

Analysis of Options

1.   She may not have understood what I was saying because my accent is different from the American accent. This is a possible answer.
2.   Words differ in usage. We say cover in India, but Americans say paper or plastic bag. Here again is another simple difference in semantics. This difficulty in these types of situations is that when people do not receive the response they were expecting they tend to make negative judgments about the other person. What is different is often perceived as wrong or rude, thus the cashier's response. This is the best answer.
3.   She might not be patient enough to handle this situation because she was tired that day.
4.   Although I might have inadvertently insulted her, that was not my intention. My tone and gestures were genuinely polite. There is a better answer.

7

For Spring break a couple of years ago my parents and I went to Australia. We got around and along just fine, but on the third night when we were in a bar having a few drinks my Dad challenged me to a game of pool. So I walked up to put my name on the chalkboard to get the next game on the pool tables. I wrote my name, and then I went back to the stool to finish my drink. When the game was over the guy that lost walked up to me and said that he was pissed. I asked him why and he looked at me in a weird way, then asked me where I was from. I told him California. He smiled and pointed to his friend. He said that his friend was really pissed. I looked and saw his friend stumbling out the bar door.

How would you explain to the American what was going on?

Options

1. The Australian was mad at the American for wanting to play pool.
2. The Australian does not like people to challenge him to pool.
3. The word pissed means something different in America than in Australia.
4. The Australian was mad about losing the game and wanted to fight the American.

Analysis of Options

1. Please choose again, I doubt that the Australian was mad at the American for wanting to play pool.
2. Wrong, the Australian was not challenged to a game of pool.
3. Yes, this is the correct answer. In Australia the word pissed means that you are drunk, whereas in America the word pissed means to be mad at someone.
4. Please choose again. He may be mad about losing, but not mad enough to fight.

8

My mother and sister were bickering as I walked in. It appeared that my mother had received an urgent call from a close friend. Her friend stated that she had suffered a serious accident at work and needed a ride home from the doctor's office. My mother's primary language is Spanish. In all actuality she only speaks English in a fight or flight situation, meaning when she is very upset or she's trying to defend her rights and halfway speaks English. Needless to say, the lack of practice of English contributes to a heavy Latin American accent in her pronunciation. Sometimes this accent can be quite challenging. On this particular day my sister was experiencing first hand the frustration of not communicating effectively.

It appears that my sister, Diane, sat for an hour waiting for my mother's friend at the doctor's parking lot. My mother had begged my sister to please pick up her friend at "Dr. Santuree's" office. After sitting in the car for some time in Dr. Century's parking lot, Diane grew upset. Then she found out that our friend was not even at that office. Diane approached my mother in complete frustration, and my mother continued to beckon for her friend's ride.

Diane was angrily looking through the phone book and calling 411 in complete frustration of not finding the doctor's office or phone number. I then decided to sit with mom and have her speak to me in a less excited tone and with clearer pronunciation. That too became tiresome, so I then asked her to write it down for me. I knew that I needed to accommodate to her linguistic needs in order to reach our goal: picking up her injured friend. In big bold letters my mother wrote DOCTORSONDUTY (Doctors on Duty). It was quite funny. My mother still did not understand what all the commotion was on our part, and she thought my sister was an absolute idiot for not understanding something as basic as "Doctors on Duty."

How could we have prevented this situation?

Options

1. Diane should have talked to my mother's friend directly.
2. Diane should have drove home to talk to my mother in person.
3. Diane should have asked my mother to spell the doctor's name.
4. Diane should have tried to be more accommodating and less angry.

Analysis of Options

1. This may not have been possible. Please choose again.
2. This would have wasted even more time and probably would have angered both Diane, my mom, and her friend. Please choose again.
3. Since Diane is aware of her mother's accent and difficulty with English, she could have prevented this problem by checking the spelling before she left. This is a possible answer.
4. One of the reasons this is such a difficult situation is that everyone became angry and frustrated. If one knows she will be dealing with an accent or foreign language, one has to expect it will take more time and require more patience. This may have prevented some of the frustration between Diane, her sister, and her mom. This is a possible answer.

9

Shunsuke, a 13-year-old boy, had to move to the United States from Japan. His father works for a Japanese firm as one of the business managers and the company had transferred him there to set up a new branch and to manage its operations thereafter. Since this was a seven-year contract with the company, Shunsuke would get the rest of his education and spend his entire teenage years in the United States. Upon arrival to the United States, he was impressed by how big everything was, the streets, the cars, the houses, and the people, compared to their counterparts back in Japan. He was worried that he might not be able to adapt to this new environment and their way of life. Also, because of the language difference, he was worried that he might have communication problems. Although he had been taking English lessons in Japan ever since he was in elementary school, and had taken English classes in Junior High, he had never come face to face with an actual live "gaijin" (foreigner). However, contrary to his worries, as he began going to his new school, he made new friends. He found that American kids were more easy going than those in Japan and were easier to get along with. He also found that the class atmosphere was more relaxed than in his home country. So he was able to adapt to his new environment and bond with his new friends rather quickly, even though he could not understand a lot of what they were saying. Soon, his new friends started asking him to come over to their house and play saying, "It wouldn't be possible for you to come over to my house today, would it?" Since Shunsuke wanted to be with his friends more and have something to do after school, he accepted the invitation and answered the invitation positively. Yet when he answered, his friends just said. "oh" and walked away. His friends asked him several times since then, and he answered them with a positive answer every time, but his friends would just walk off after he answered. Soon, his friends did not ask him anymore. Shunsuke was confused; here he was telling them that he wanted to play, but his friends kept walking away without making any further plans, and nothing ever happened.

How can you explain this situation to Shunsuke?

Options

1. Although Shunsuke answered them positively, his facial expression suggested otherwise. His friends interpreted this as non-verbal language as a "no," thinking that Shunsuke really did not want to be with them. (In Japan, it is a communication rule to make a facial expression to mean something opposite of what you say, and this is what caused the miscommunication.)
2. His friends meant for the invitation to be a casual one and did not really mean "come over *today.*" In contrast, to Shunsuke, when someone says something, they really mean it in a literal way. In Japan, people take other people's words literally, but in the United States, invitations have a more casual meaning. The problem was that he incorrectly decoded the meaning for the word "today."
3. In Japan, when someone asks you "It wouldn't be possible, would it?", and you want to give them a positive answer meaning "yes, it is possible," they say "no" meaning "no, it *is* possible." Hence, when Shunsuke meant to give his friends a positive answer, in actuality, he gave them an answer that had a negative meaning to them. It is this difference in the grammar of language that caused the misinterpretation.
4. His friends didn't like Orientals and were just teasing him to make him feel bad.

Analysis of Options

1. This is not the case. Although nonverbal communication differs greatly from culture to culture, there is no communication rule in Japan that says to make the opposite facial expression to what you say. Facial expression in Japan can be subtle, but usually fits into the context accordingly.

2. This is not the case. There is a so-called "casual invitation" in Japan also, and the way to determine if an invitation is a casual one or a real one is the same as in the United States. Therefore, since he knew how to tell these apart, he must have known that the invitation was not just a casual "whenever" type invitation.

3. This is the best answer. It is true that when you ask a question such as, "It wouldn't be possible, would it?" in Japanese, people would reply, "it *is* possible" meaning "yes" in English. In Japan, the question, "It wouldn't be possible, would it?" is thought to contain a negative word or a "no" to make a positive answer "yes." This is simply a matter of *syntactics*, or language structure.

4. Obviously, this is not the case.

10

I work in sales for a large dating service. In my consultations I spend about a half an hour getting to know the potential member, and about another 20 minutes telling them about how the service works. One day, I had a consultation scheduled with a man named Manesh. After talking to him, I found out that he was originally from India and had been in the Bay Area for about 7 months. He had gotten a job here and was planning on staying in the area for some time. After talking to him about himself for quite a while, we started talking about what kind of woman he would like to meet. He went into great detail about physical aspects. Whenever I probed for more inner qualities, he would answer some questions but mostly said that it didn't really matter.

I proceeded to tell him all about how our program works and how easy it would be for him to find the type of woman he was looking for with the pictures, videos, and profile forms. He was very pleased that he got to see pictures of the women and thought that we were very high class to provide videos too. He also liked that he got to choose the women, that they wouldn't be picked out for him.

When I told him about the memberships and prices, he was appalled that our service cost so much to meet a woman, and got up to leave.

What happened?

Options

1. Manesh was playing a practical joke to see what my reaction would be.
2. Having just recently moved, Manesh didn't have enough money to be able to afford the service, and was insulted that I didn't tell him right away what the prices were.
3. Manesh felt that I hadn't explained the program in enough detail because I would not show him pictures of the woman we had available, so he'd be going into it blindly.
4. Manesh misunderstood what our service was and thought it was an escort service.

Analysis of Options

1. Although this does happen from time to time, Manesh was so enthused by the service during the consultation, this didn't seem like a good explanation.
2. This could be a possibility. I did try to go over that in the beginning while finding out about his life, but there could have been a reason that he didn't want to divulge his personal financial information to me.
3. This is highly doubtful, because I do make it fairly clear from the beginning that it is a confidential dating service, and that we only show pictures and profiles to other members.
4. This is what happened. After Manesh got up to leave, I had him sit down so we could talk about what upset him. I found out that he was already promised to someone for marriage, so he wasn't at all interested in or available for a "relationship" in the way that I was talking about. Our language barrier and interpretation of words caused us to have crossed signals. Although we were talking about two entirely different things, in the consultation we both thought we were talking about the same thing. We both had a good laugh about it and parted with a better understanding of each other's diverse backgrounds.

11

My friend had recently arrived from India. He and his American girlfriend and a group of friends from various other countries, including myself, were studying in a library. My friend and his girlfriend were busy drawing diagrams with a pencil. He asked his girlfriend if she can "please pass his rubber." His girlfriend felt insulted in front of everyone else. She abruptly gathered her books and walked away before anyone realized. They were never friends again and my friend lost his chance to explain.

What should the girl have done?

Options

1. She could have ignored his comments.
2. She could have asked any other Indian sitting in that group what it meant.
3. She could have passed the "rubber."
4. The girl should have immediately demanded an explanation or asked him to point it to her.

Analysis of Options

1. This is highly possible. She could have ignored his comments but then he innocently not knowing would have repeated his request and she would be in the same position again.
2. This is possible but not feasible. She could have asked others who were sitting there but then it would have been better asking the person himself.
3. This is not possible. She did not know what "rubber" in India meant and so could not pass it.
4. This is the most appropriate response. She could have asked him what it meant or how dare he say that and he would have either pointed to his eraser or explained to her that in India "rubber" is what a pencil eraser is to the U.S. Unfortunately most people don't ask for explanations, they simply cut off the communication as the girlfriend did here. This is a phenomenon called *autistic hostility*, and it seriously damages relationships.

12

Three years after I first came to the U.S., I met my boyfriend. He left Vietnam as a young boy of seven years old, and, at the time, had lived abroad for about 20 years. Our very first conversation on the phone was interrupted and finally ended because of his sister's call on the waiting line. The last phrase I heard from him was, "I'll talk to you later." I waited and waited but he did not call me back right away as I expected. After waiting for three hours, I thought he might have forgotten to call me back, so I picked up the phone to call him, only to find out from his parents that he had gone to his friend's party. Although I was very upset, I asked his parents politely to leave him a message that I called and that I would like him to call me back at whatever time that he got home. He got home at 2:00 A.M. and he called me. He was very shocked to find out that I picked up the phone at the first ring and that I was anxiously waiting for his call.

"You told me that you'll talk to me *later*," I accused him.

"I said that I'll talk to you *later*, as in tomorrow or the day after," argued Joseph.

Why did I misunderstand?

Options

1. I expected him to spend all his time talking to me.
2. I did understand correctly, but he was just avoiding me.
3. Even though we speak the same language, words have different meanings.
4. He didn't say what he meant.

Analysis of Options

1. This is unrealistic. It was our very first telephone conversation.
2. There is no evidence of this. In fact, he called me as soon as he got the message, even though it was 2:00 A.M. It's unlikely he was avoiding me.
3. In the Vietnamese language, 'later' usually means a short period of time, mostly on a same day basis. Thus, I was a victim of my own interpretation of the word 'later.' I could have confirmed with Joseph, "Oh, do you mean tomorrow or next week?" However, because of the difference in our cultures, even though both of us were born in the same country, we have a different understanding of the same word and that was why we miscommunicated all together.
4. Another possible solution is that Joseph could be more specific about his timing, like, "I'll call you some other time." 'Some other time' is definitely less vague than 'later.' By saying this he would eliminate the possibility of a misunderstanding from my part and I would not expect him to call me back in a short period after we hung up. This option requires that he would be able to anticipate misunderstandings, which may not be practical.

13

The sun was shining, and the sunbeams were playing in the fountain's water when Olga sat down on a bench under a tree and enjoyed her lunch. She was an international student in the U.S., and eager to make new friends. Next to her sat a young Filipino student, Ray, and they started to talk. Olga, who was a Swede, was excited because she had been to the Philippines, and she told the other student about one very beautiful island that she had visited. Olga's focus was on how well she liked the natural way people were living. The community on the island was small, and everybody knew everybody. The island had only had electricity for about two years, and there were no cars, no pavements or concrete on the island. In the evenings people met at a local pub and watched TV together because not many people on the island had their own TV, Olga told Ray. On weekends the locals and the tourists went to the one dance place, a wooden floor on the beach with the sky and the stars as the ceiling. There were no supermarkets on the island, so the commerce took place on the market street where the locals sold and bought what they needed. Olga told Ray that she also went to Manila, but that she thought that it was a big and crowded city. She preferred a more quiet way of life. Ray knew about the island, and agreed that it was a wonderful place. Then Ray told Olga about a gigantic shopping center that his sister in the Philippines lived close to. The place was huge, five floors of shops, restaurants, and all kinds of entertainment. Ray continued to talk about the exclusive things in the shopping center until the lunch break was over and the two students had to say good bye. Olga left with a feeling that the conversation turned out to be a misunderstanding.

What do you think happened?

Options

1. Ray thought that Olga had gone to the Philippines to shop, and that she was disappointed that she had not found a good shopping center.
2. Ray was insulted because Olga didn't know about the huge shopping center that he told her about.
3. Ray wanted to tell Olga, in a polite and indirect way, that not every part of the Philippines is like the island that she described.
4. Ray was an enthusiastic shopper, and loved to tell other people about it.

Analysis of Options

1. This is not the best choice. Olga did not say that she liked to shop. On the contrary, she told him that she liked the natural way of life.
2. This answer is partly correct. Ray might have felt insulted, but not because Olga didn't know about this specific shopping center. He understood that she couldn't possibly know about it since she had not been there. But Ray could feel insulted because he felt that Olga thought that the Philippines is an underdeveloped country. But there is a better explanation for this misunderstanding.
3. This is the best answer. As a Filipino, Ray didn't want to tell Olga directly that many places in the Philippines are just as civilized as, for example, Silicon Valley in the U.S. Instead, he told her about the mall so that she would understand that fact for herself. By telling Olga this in a direct way would contradict the Filipino culture where you don't want people to "lose their face." Ray didn't want to insult Olga.
4. We are not told whether or not Ray likes to shop. Even if he does, this fact would not explain the strange feeling Olga got after the conversation. There are more complex answers for this situation. Try again!

14

During the course of my employment as a technical placement specialist I encountered many different people of Asian descent. I am an English speaking, U.S. American woman from a low context culture. Many of the persons I encountered were primarily Chinese or Korean speaking Asian Americans from high context cultures. While interviewing a Chinese gentleman one afternoon I found myself becoming very frustrated with this man because of communication barriers. The man did not speak English very well, and I did not speak Chinese. The man was not able to answer the questions I asked about his employment history, and he couldn't tell me why he wanted the position that was available. I looked at my watch to give a signal that the interview was drawing to a close, and the gentleman did not recognize this attempt to end this interview. After several more minutes I was able to end the interview. The gentleman asked me if he would be interviewing with the other employee in the office, who happened to be a man. When I informed the gentleman that he would not be interviewing with the other man in the office, a look of confusion came over his face and he left the office.

What would you do in this situation?

Options

1. Talk louder so the man could understand you.
2. Do not give this man a position in the company because he did not speak English well.
3. Ask the man to come back to another interview with an interpreter.
4. Allow more time for the interview and explain expectations.

Analysis of Options

1. This is not a very good choice. The man is having difficulty understanding and being understood, not hearing or being heard. Talking louder may appear that you are angry or hostile toward the man.
2. This would be a very bad decision to make. Because a person does not speak the language you speak, does not mean that they are unqualified for a position. If the man found out that he did not get a position in the company because of his language differences he may view this as discrimination and sue the company.
3. Asking the man to come back with an interpreter might be a good idea. You would need to do it in a manner that wouldn't offend him.
4. The best answer is to allow more time for the interview. By allowing more time for the interview you would be able to speak more slowly and clearly. The Chinese organizational and logic preference is extremely different from that of the U.S. American. The preferred style in China is to digress into many related areas, whereas the U.S. American style is to be more direct and to the point. The Chinese person is likely to think that the U.S American is rude and aggressive. Conversely, the U.S. American is likely to view the Chinese American as confusing and imprecise. Both people in this critical incident are likely to feel dissatisfied, confused and uncomfortable if more time and understanding of cultural differences are not taken into consideration. Furthermore, because of this difference in logic preference, it would be helpful for the interviewer to explain his or her expectations up front, thus decreasing the likelihood of misunderstanding.

15

I went to the store to get my medication and an Asian woman, who is the manager, helped me. She had a very heavy accent and I found it very hard to understand her. I gave her my prescription, and she told me it would take five minutes. I went back after five minutes, and she told me there was a problem, but that everything would be fine. I waited for another 10 minutes and she kept telling me everything would be fine and to hold on. Finally, another person came around and gave me my medication and explained the situation. My name had been deleted from the system. I was so angry and so late I just grabbed my medication and left.

Why did she keep telling me that everything would be fine?

Options

1. She broke the computer and didn't want anyone else to find out.
2. She didn't know how to use the computer.
3. She is from a high context culture and was trying to fix the problem the best way she knew how.
4. She had a long line of others waiting for her to help them.

Analysis of Options

1. The computer system wasn't broken; it just had an error. Choose again.
2. She has to know how to use the computer system if she is the manager. Choose again.
3. She is from a high context culture and she was doing everything she could to fix it. I found out later that she had someone in the back room calling the company and that she was talking to another manager to get information. She apparently thought that she had conveyed a direct message, but it was very high context and very indirect. She also probably felt that she had given me the information that I needed, that everything would be fine, without realizing that I needed more information to justify such a large amount of my time being taken.
4. There was no mention of a line. Please choose again.

16

I was born in New Jersey and moved to Southern California when I was a freshman in high school. One day I returned to school with a new hair style and a friend said to me, "Your hair looks BAD." Needless to say I felt awful. Here I had someone tell me right to my face that my hair looked bad. I think I responded by saying, "really" with a very surprised look on my face. I saw another friend in my next class and I told her what had happened and she laughed at me and I think I may have cried. She said that "BAD" means good. Well, how was I supposed to know that? This was a slang word that resembled "really good." After this occurred, I asked her explain all of the slang in her vocabulary, because I certainly did not want this to happen again, and she did.

How could I have prevented this situation?

Options

1. I should have realized that I was in a new culture and meanings would be different.
2. I should have confronted the issue at the time so that I had a better understanding of the situation.
3. I could have asked about some of the slang terms before I found myself in this situation.
4. I should not have taken the word literally and should have thought that most people would not be so up front with you, and therefore "BAD" must have meant something else.

Analysis of Options

1. Number one is the best explanation because I should have realized that cultures vary and maybe there was something I didn't know. Although I was still in the United States, New Jersey culture is very different from California culture. Therefore differences in communication between these two areas are also great. Being aware of that would have prevented the hurt feelings and allowed me to find out the real meaning of the word "bad."
2. Number two was a good explanation because if I confronted the situation I would have learned sooner that the comment did not literally mean bad. I could have asked for clarification.
3. This is unrealistic. I wouldn't know what to ask about.
4. This is a possibility. A good intercultural strategy is to assume the best about misunderstandings. One would think that people would not be so up front about something that they know would hurt your feelings. This was not something I was experiencing with others from that culture so it would have seemed abnormal for my friend to make this comment directly to me. However, this strategy does not help me determine what "bad" means.

17

My friend, Dung and I were talking with each other about our math homework. Sitting next to us was Jack, one of Dung's American friends. He was also in our math class. I was showing Dung how to do one of the problems. We used to talk to each other in Vietnamese because it is easier to understand each other. After finishing our work, we started talking about some jokes that I saw in the newspaper. We laughed our hearts out. In the middle of our conversation, Jack quietly stood up and left without saying a word. I noticed that Jack was gone when we were ready to leave for class. I asked Dung why Jack had left, and he just shrugged his shoulders and off we went.

Why did Jack leave?

Options

1. Jack thought that he had no business staying there because he did not get any reaction from us.
2. Jack may be offended because we did not ask him advice about the math problem.
3. Jack doesn't like the sound of foreign languages.
4. Jack felt bad because he thought that we were talking about him and did not want him to know.

Analysis of Options

1. Since we sat with Jack the common language that we should have used was English rather than Vietnamese, because it makes it easier for everyone to understand and does not leave anyone out. Jack probably felt that his presence was not desired. People use language to identify with a group of people. When an unfamiliar language is spoken, people feel like they do not belong. They become *outgroup members* instead of *ingroup members*. This is the best answer.
2. While getting him involved in the math problem is a good way to start a conversation, there is nothing in the story to indicate that Jack wanted to help solve the problem. Choose again.
3. There is nothing in the story to indicate this. Choose again.
4. This is a possible answer. Jack may have believed he was being talked about. Often when communicating with people from other cultures people feel insecure. Such insecurities combined with a foreign language can frequently lead to suspicions of being talked about. However, there is also another possibility.

18

In high school John had a Japanese girlfriend, Junko. One night he went to her house for dinner so he could meet her grandparents. As they sat down at the dinner table, Junko's grandparents and mother started speaking Japanese and would look at John occasionally. In the mean time John asked Junko how her day was going. After dinner they had coffee and Junko's mother asked him to stay over for a movie. John refused and left abruptly after finishing his coffee, giving no excuse.

Why did John leave so soon?

Options

1. He left because he did not understand Junko's mother.
2. He was annoyed because Junko's family did not make an attempt to communicate verbally or nonverbally.
3. He felt it was alright for them to speak another language because it's the only language they know, but was bored with little conversation.
4. John had a lot of homework and was stressed.

Analysis of Options

1. There is nothing to indicate her English was not clear. Please choose again.
2. This is a good answer. John wanted to be involved, but could not because of the language barrier. Junko's mother's request for John to stay for a movie was in English, emphasizing his frustration at being left out of the rest of the conversation. As in the previous incident, Junko's mother's choice to speak Japanese instead of English made John feel like an outgroup member and not welcome.
3. While John may have been bored, a movie could remedy that. There is a better answer to explain his sudden departure.
4. There is no mention of homework in the story. Please choose again.

19

The culture episode that I am going to write about happened in my senior year in high school. I transferred high schools in my senior year from a private school, Mitty High School, to a San Jose Unified, public school. At Pioneer High School they bussed in a lot of English as a second language students of Mexican descent. This was really different for me coming from a predominantly White school. Well I wanted to take it easy my senior year and not have to worry about much except for enjoying my last year of high school and playing basketball and baseball and hopefully excelling in those. My baseball coach asked me if I wanted to be his teaching assistant for his PE class he was teaching, He told me that I wouldn't have to do much and it would be an easy grade. This was cool, most of the time I just sat in his office and chilled or I would teach the younger students PE. My coach gave me full control. The thing I didn't know was that half the class didn't speak English. Well, of the twenty or so kids that didn't speak English about ten of them were really difficult and wouldn't do anything that me or the teachers would say; they would swear at us in Spanish and disrupt the class. I dealt with it by having to take them to OCS on campus suspension. They hated the teacher and me for it, and I hated them. I felt like physically beating them sometimes they would make me so mad, but now I realize that I should have tried to relate to them because it was hard enough for them being in a school where not many people understood them and made them outcasts. But they also did it to themselves by taunting and being obnoxious to the other students in the school.

Why didn't I get along with these students?

Options
1. This was a case where both sides just didn't understand each other and that caused both sides to have bitter feelings and act out the way they did.
2. The people involved just did not like each other.
3. Cultural prejudice caused both sides not to like each other and be unfair to one another.
4. It was just ten or so kids who didn't like school and were acting out during their PE class, and they were just not very well mannered kids.

Analysis of Options
1. I feel this was a case where the language barriers and both sides not understanding each other caused the kids to act out. Because they did not speak English, they were ostracized by the rest of the kids. This was probably a very stressful situation to be in, so these students probably felt angry, frustrated, and bitter. Unfortunately, these emotions tend to destroy effective communication.
2. Since we didn't speak the same language, we had difficulty even getting to know one another. There is a better option.
3. Although both sides may not have believed that they were prejudiced, people do tend to react negatively to an unfamiliar language. As humans, we're attracted to similarities in people, not usually differences. This may be a factor, but there is a better answer.
4. There is more going on here than just manners. Choose again.

20

Francisco's family immigrated to America from Spain, so the whole family was fluent in Spanish and English. After dating Francisco for a few months, he finally introduced me to his mother. Immediately after our introduction she asked, "do you speak Spanish?" I explained that two years of high school Spanish was the limit to my knowledge of the language. "Too bad," she replied and left the room.

Why did she leave the room?

Options

1. She left because she suddenly remembered something she had to do.
2. She did not want her son dating someone who was not fluent in Spanish.
3. She disliked speaking English and would rather have Spanish spoken in her home.
4. She is upset that her son did not introduce her to his girlfriend in Spanish.

Analysis of Options

1. This is possible, but unlikely. She gave no indication that something of importance came up.
2. While this is partially correct, there is a better answer for her departure.
3. This is the best answer. Francisco's mother felt awkward speaking English and preferred that only Spanish be spoken in her home. People are often apprehensive about speaking in a new language, but it doesn't necessarily mean that she didn't want to communicate with me. She may just have been disappointed that we couldn't carry on a conversation as easily.
4. There is no indication in the story that this is what Francisco's mother expected.

21

During the spring of last year, my old childhood playmates came from the Philippines to visit me. Their names were Andrew and Clarice. I was really looking forward to seeing them and I was ready to ask them a lot of questions about "back home." I also looked forward to reminiscing about the old days.

Upon their arrival, I greeted them with a big smile. "Hi!" I said. "How are you?"

Andrew and Clarice smiled a little and returned my greeting with quiet "hello's."

I asked them plenty of questions and tried to make them feel comfortable, but nothing seemed to work. Andrew and Clarice just sat quietly on my couch. Every time I'd ask them questions such as "How was your flight?" or "Are you enjoying your tour of the country?" they would give me short answers. They even seemed reluctant to talk to me.

At that point, I could not help but think that I must be doing something wrong. These were not the same boisterous, fun-loving playmates I had remembered them to be. It seemed that Andrew and Clarice did not want to talk to me. They weren't as excited as I was.

What would help explain this awkward situation?

Options

1. Andrew and Clarice were annoyed by my perkiness.
2. Andrew and Clarice were not as excited about the reunion because they didn't really consider me a good friend.
3. Andrew and Clarice were a little shy talking to me.
4. I was obviously failing as a hostess and did not have good hostess skills.

Analysis of Options

1. It's possible, but there is no evidence that Andrew and Clarice were annoyed.
2. This is not possible because it wouldn't explain the fact that they had wanted to visit me in the first place.
3. This is the best possible answer. They were shy about talking to me because they were afraid that I would make fun of their English speaking skills. Although English is taught in Philippine schools, Andrew and Clarice were not comfortable speaking English all the time. So I made the effort in speaking to them in Tagalog, their native language. When I did that, I too was a little scared that they would make fun of me because I didn't know that much Tagalog. But it was only when I tried to speak to them in the language they were more familiar with that I began to completely understand the awkward position that they were in.
4. This may also be possible, but there is no evidence to support this answer.

22

Rohit is one of my Indian friends who went to high school with me. Rohit and I share many interests such as dancing, music, video games, movies, and sense of humor. When we hang out together we have a good time, just the two of us. However, one day I went over Rohit's house to find that we were going to spend the day with a friend he knew from his old high school. His friend's name was Parag, and he was Indian also. I had no problem with Parag because he was cool, talking about music and things like that. However, Rohit and Parag often engaged in speaking Hindi, an Indian dialect. When they would laugh about something, I would just kind of chuckle even though I had no idea what they were laughing about. Usually when I'm with Rohit, I am very talkative. But when Parag was around I was very quiet. Rohit didn't notice my uneasiness, but I was uncomfortable and ready to go home.

How would you interpret my disappointment?

Options

1. Rohit was trying to hide something by speaking in his native tongue.
2. I was being selfish, thinking that I was receiving less attention from Rohit.
3. Rohit felt that I don't know anything about the events that happened during his years at his old high school, so he assumes that I don't need to hear about them.
4. It's very natural for Rohit to speak in Hindi because it is his home language and he is accustomed to speaking Hindi to Indians regardless of who is around.

Analysis of Options

1. This answer is way off. I was Rohit's friend. Anything Rohit could say to Parag, Rohit could say to me.
2. It is true the I would receive less attention from Rohit, but I must take into consideration that Rohit hasn't seen his friend for a long time, and when Indians don't see each other for a while, they make an event out of it when they do see each other. This isn't the right answer.
3. Although I didn't go to Rohit's old high school, I'm sure Rohit wouldn't mind filling me in on some of the funny events that happened to Rohit and Parag. In fact, I might get a kick out of hearing the stories, and Rohit might get a kick out of telling them to me. Try again.
4. This is the right answer. Rohit naturally speaks to Indians in Hindi regardless of who is around. Rohit felt more comfortable speaking to Parag in Hindi because at his old high school, that's all Rohit and Parag spoke to each other. Also, Rohit is more comfortable speaking in his native tongue since his English isn't perfect. Moreover, Rohit liked to hold on to his customs no matter where he was in the world. My problem was that I was used to Rohit speaking English to me. Also, neither I nor the friends that Rohit and I hung out with spoke Hindi. Therefore, there wouldn't be a need for Rohit to speak any other language than English on other occasions.

Comments

When one begins to look at language differences, one salient issue is *semantics*. Semantics are the rules that govern meaning. They are the practical applications of a word. Therefore, even when people are speaking the same language, meanings are often misunderstood such as in incidents #5–12 and #16. Although we usually do not pay attention to semantic issues until a misunderstanding has occurred, it is helpful to remember that meanings are in the people who use the words, not in the words themselves. Ogden and Richards illustrate this concept through their *Triangle of Meaning*. In the model below, they demonstrate that the user (the one who is sending a message) is the one who decides which symbols (words, signs, and nonverbal communication) will represent their referents (thoughts and ideas). Hence, meaning is ultimately decided by the user.

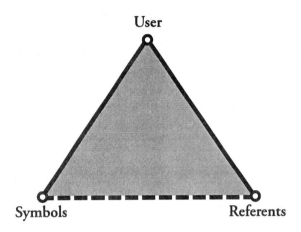

Furthermore, these incidents also present us with classic examples of the difficulty of interaction between *high context* and *low context* cultures. According to Hall (1976), a *high context culture* is one that emphasizes implied meaning. In other words, high context people will use fewer words and more nonverbal communication in order to hint at their meaning. To fully understand a high context person, one must understand the cultural rules that go along with the communication and the relevance of the social context. A low context culture, however, is just the opposite. In a *low context culture*, the emphasis is on directness. Consequently, communication is explicit and direct, leaving little to the imagination. These differences are illustrated in incidents #1 and 13–15.

Therefore, someone who prefers a high context style would consider explicitness and directness to be overly stating the obvious, and thus condescending and rude. Additionally, many high context cultures avoid the use of the negative (i.e., saying no) because it is considered too direct and impolite. Consequently, one must read between the lines to understand when "yes" may mean "no." Of course, someone who prefers a low context style would consider such indirectness vague and uncooperative.

These types of judgments often lead to *fundamental attribution error* (Ross, 1977). Attributions are the judgments we make about ourselves and others. In intercultural communication, we often make incorrect attributions because we do not understand the other person's culture, resulting in fundamental attribution error. In addition to the emotional issues primarily involved with attributions we also have the difficulty of getting across the correct information, resulting in frustration and frequently anger as we can see in incident #2.

Thus, our student's analysis in incident #1 is correct. When placed in a position where receiving accurate information is vital, one must use *open-ended questions* that require respondents to give details. Even then, one must still be aware of the nonverbal cues. Do they contradict what the person is saying verbally? Does the person seem uncomfortable? Does the person look like they may have more information to get across? All these subtleties may not be said, but are often easily seen in facial expression or heard in tone of voice if one is observant. Competent communicators will not just look for the message, but will also watch for nonverbal cues and try to understand the context of the situation.

However, understanding the context of the situation is difficult if one is not a member of the ingroup. According to Triandis (1988), an *ingroup* is a group that is important to its members. It is a group that one feels a sense of belonging to. Ingroup members, therefore, will understand the context of the situation and be better equipped to interpret nuances of the conversation and subtle nonverbal messages than someone who is not a member of that particular group. Consequently, when people are communicating interculturally, by definition they are not members of the same group. Thus, in depth understanding between a high context person and a low context person becomes difficult. The importance of groups is illustrated in incidents #18–20 and #22.

One additional variable that can create an obstacle to intercultural communication is *organization of thought.* Some cultures prefer a linear, direct organization, focusing on clarity for the receiver of the message. Others prefer a less direct, often implied organization, shifting the responsibility for understanding to the listener. Still others may prefer a more roundabout style, touching on related issues and eventually reaching the main idea. As listeners, we instinctively pay attention to the organizational style that we prefer. The difficulty in that practice is when the speaker does not use the preferred style listeners tend to tune out, assuming that the main idea is never coming because it did not come when expected. Clearly, this leads to miscommunication.

As you can see, there are many variables involved even with subtle language differences. Awareness of these potential obstacles to communication will enhance your communication with people from a diversity of cultures.

_____ Language Exercises _____

Exercise 1. The Rugby / Bowling Challenge

Piper McNulty, De Anza College, Cupertino, California

I. Challenge #1

A. Identifying Your Natural Conversation Style:

1. _(After viewing the video(s)):_ * Consider the context of _classroom discussion_ with your peers (classmates). Which of the two global conversational styles, rugby and bowling, is closest to _your natural style in this context_? Circle the number that corresponds to your natural style.

Rugby   1   2   3   4   5   6   7   8   9   10   Bowling

2. Which ethnic cultures have shaped your socialization? _____

_____

3. Do you think that your natural style stems from your cultural socialization, or is idiosyncratic?

cultural socialization / idiosyncratic

B. Brainstorming Behaviors:

Working in a small group, or in whole class discussion, develop a list of the specific communication behaviors which seem to demonstrate each style. _(IM)_ Record these here:

Bowling:	Rugby:
_____ _never interrupt_ _____	_____ _interrupt_ _____
_____	_____
_____	_____
_____	_____
_____	_____
_____	_____
_____	_____

* See Instructor's Manual

C. Identifying Your Target Conversational Style:

1.   Now you will choose your *target* conversational style. Look back at I-A above. Where did you mark yourself on the continuum? Choose the style *farthest* from your natural style as your target. If you marked a 4, 5 or 6 in I-A above, your target style could be either rugby or bowling. If this is the case, consider your target culture (the culture you interact with, or will be interacting with, which is most different from your own). Pick the conversational style which is most like the style which people in your target culture typically demonstrate. Ask the instructor for advice if you cannot decide which style to choose as your target style, or if you are not sure which style is dominant in your target culture.

2.   For your target style, from the list of behaviors in (B) above, *mark two behaviors* which you will attempt to demonstrate. These will be your *target behaviors* in the practice which follows.

D. Practice and Feedback (IM)

1.   You will participate in a small group discussion with your team. The instructor will assign a discussion topic. Your team will have 5 minutes to discuss this topic using the *bowling* style, and then five minutes to continue discussing the same topic using the *rugby* style. *(IM)*

2.   During this discussion, you will be trying to consistently demonstrate your target conversational (bowling or rugby). Below, write down the style you will challenge (your "Target Style"), and two behaviors from this style which you will try to demonstrate (Target Behaviors).

My Target Style: (circle one) Rugby / Bowling

Target Behaviors:	Feedback Received:
a. _____	a. _____ _____
b. _____	b. _____ _____

3.   While your team discusses the topic the instructor chooses, your feedback partner will be keeping a careful record of how often and how effectively you demonstrate your target behaviors. After your team's discussion, on the lines above, copy down the feedback you receive from your feedback partner.

4.   Write down the following for your feedback partner:

Partner's Name: _____

Partner's Target Style (circle one): Rugby / Bowling

Partner's Target Behaviors:	Feedback for Partner: *(based on observations of partner during his/her team's discussion)*
a. _____	a. _____ _____
b. _____	b. _____ _____

After your partner's discussion is finished, give him/her feedback using the notes you have made in (4) above.

E. Continued Practice

As appropriate, practice your target conversational style in interactions with classmates, colleagues and friends. Your goal is to become as effective as possible at matching the style of your various conversation partners throughout the day.

II. Challenge #2 *(several weeks later)*

A. Practice and Feedback

1.   You will participate in a small group discussion with your team (new topic). Your team will have 5 minutes to discuss this topic using the *bowling* style, and five minutes to continue discussing the same topic using the *rugby* style.

2.   This time, during this discussion, *all* students, regardless of natural style and target style, will demonstrate the bowling style, and then *all* students will demonstrate the rugby style.

For *each* style, select *3* target behaviors. List them here, and tell your partner which behaviors you have chosen.

My Target Behaviors:

Bowling:	Feedback Received:
a. _____	a. _____ _____
b. _____	b. _____ _____
c. _____	c. _____ _____

Rugby:	Feedback Received:
a. _____	a. _____ _____
b. _____	b. _____ _____
c. _____	c. _____ _____

Partner's Target Behaviors:

Bowling:	Feedback Received:
a. _____	a. _____
	_____
b. _____	b. _____
	_____
c. _____	c. _____
	_____

Rugby:	Feedback Received:
a. _____	a. _____
	_____
b. _____	b. _____
	_____
c. _____	c. _____
	_____

Observe and give feedback as before.

III. Challenge #3 *(several weeks later)*

A. Practice and Feedback

1.   You will participate in a small group discussion with your team (new topic). As before, your team will have 5 minutes to discuss this topic using the *bowling* style, and five minutes to continue discussing the same topic using the *rugby* style.

2.   During this discussion, *every* student on your team, regardless of natural style, will demonstrate the *bowling* style, and then *every* student will demonstrate the *rugby* style. *This time you will try to demonstrate **all** the behaviors listed below.* Record the feedback your partner gives you.

Feedback Received from Partner

Bowling:	Feedback Received:
Never interrupt a team member.	
Wait one full second ("one Mississippi") after someone else has finished speaking.	
Scan your teammates' faces. Do not speak if someone else looks as though they might want to speak.	
Gatekeep (encourage others to speak. Use a respectful, unchallenging tone: "What do *you* think?")	
Do not challenge or criticize others' ideas.	
If you must disagree, first say "yes" to acknowledge the other person's idea, then state your own idea.	
Keep your facial expression pleasant or neutral.	
Avoid fidgeting or other non-verbal signals of impatience or disagreement. Keep your body still.	
Use back channeling (supportive listening noises) to encourage other speakers.	
Do not "hog the floor." Do not speak more than 2–3 sentences before allowing others to speak. Do not start speaking again till someone else has spoken even if there is a lengthy silence.	
Do not raise your voice. Maintain a calm tone.	

Rugby:	Feedback Received:
Interrupt. If you need thinking time, use interrupting noises (ah, . . . well . . .) to gain and hold the floor till you can decide what to say. Do not allow any silence. Use animated hand gestures and facial expressions Disagree freely and directly. Raise your voice if necessary to hold your turn or to show how strongly you feel about something. Use strong non-verbal signals to indicate that you want to speak (lean forward in your chair, touch others on the arm, open your mouth as if to speak).	_____ _____ _____ _____ _____ _____ _____ _____ _____ _____ _____ _____

Feedback for Partner

Bowling:	Feedback for Partner:
Never interrupt a team member. Wait one full second ("one Mississippi") after someone else has finished speaking. Scan your teammates' faces. Do not speak if someone else looks as though they might want to speak. Gatekeep (encourage others to speak. Use a respectful, unchallenging tone: "What do *you* think?") Do not challenge or criticize others' ideas. If you must disagree, first say "yes" to acknowledge the other person's idea, then state your own idea. Keep your facial expression pleasant or neutral. Avoid fidgeting or other non-verbal signals of impatience or disagreement. Keep your body still. Use back channeling (supportive listening noises) to encourage other speakers. Do not "hog the floor." Do not speak more than 2–3 sentences before allowing others to speak. Do not start speaking again till someone else has spoken even if there is a lengthy silence. Do not raise your voice. Maintain a calm tone.	

Rugby:	Feedback Recorded:
Interrupt. If you need thinking time, use interrupting noises (ah, . . . well . . .) to gain and hold the floor till you can decide what to say.	_____
	_____
Do not allow any silence.	_____
	_____
Use animated hand gestures and facial expressions	_____
	_____
Disagree freely and directly.	_____
	_____
Raise your voice if necessary to hold your turn or to show how strongly you feel about something.	_____
	_____
Use strong non-verbal signals to indicate that you want to speak (lean forward in your chair, touch others on the arm, open your mouth as if to speak).	_____
	_____

Exercise 2. Personal Assessment Questions

A. Identify your communication style. Are you high or low context? Describe three characteristics of your communication style that helped you make your determination.

1. _____

2. _____

3. _____

B. Determine the communication style of the people around you. Do you notice any similarities?

_____

_____

_____

_____

_____

_____

C. Pay attention to the communication styles of both the men and women in your life. Do you notice any differences? Similarities?

_____

_____

_____

_____

_____

_____

D. Find five examples of words with a negative connotation and list their positive counterparts.

1. _____

2. _____

3. _____

4. _____

5. _____

Exercise 3. Cultural Partner Questions

It is likely your partner had to learn American English before coming to this community. If so, what difficulties did your partner have learning English? Ask your partner to describe his or her communication style. Is this style different from the norm in your community? Has it created any problems for your partner?

Chapter Two

Nonverbal Communication

23

On my first trip abroad, I landed in Amsterdam, The Netherlands. Being 18 and "green" to the travel scene, especially the kind of travel where you are not on vacation but on National Geographic, I didn't know what to expect. I reasoned that the difference couldn't be too dramatic because after all we are all human. I was correct in my assumption except in the area of sexuality as it pertains to nudity.

I was at a hostel the first evening I was there when I began to suspect that something was amiss. I couldn't determine if the shower and toilet area was for women or men. I reasoned that there might be another one out of sight in some part of the building where I didn't expect it to be, and that the one before me had the sign missing for whatever reason. Anyway, I was desperate for a shower (I'd been on a plane for 11 hours), and in my desperation to feel clean, I rationalized that I picked the right one. It was early evening, so I was alone while pondering my dilemma. Anyway, no sooner had I removed my clothes and jumped in the shower (a big open area) than a group of four women arrived, proceeded to strip and shower also. In my panic I thought that they perhaps had not noticed that I was male due to my facing the corner and their chattering. I thought that they might scream at any moment, and I would get into trouble far away from home like my parents had envisioned. I didn't even finish, although I stood in the water for what seemed an eternity. I finally mustered the courage to leave, and as I passed them I muttered a meek hello (I don't know why I even made a sound, perhaps to seem less alarming or maybe apologetic—I don't know). They responded and without, to my surprise, any expletives or attempts to conceal themselves. Perhaps they all immediately realized my mistake and allowed me to save face. I raced over to my stuff in a desperate attempt to make a quick exit when I realized that I had packed everything but a towel! I found myself cursing out loud as I tried to put on my clothes over a wet body when one of the girls handed me her towel, leaving herself exposed. I was stunned and in shock as I mechanically reached out and accepted the towel. I then quickly dried off, handed back the towel and left quickly.

It was later that I transgressed when I saw her at a bar. She said hello, and I figured that if she had been so open earlier that maybe that was a direct hint that she wanted me in a sexual way. So I proceeded to come on too strongly. To make a long story short (and without the explicit dialogue), she didn't like my approach, and let me know in no uncertain terms.

Why did I misunderstand her actions?

Options

1. She was playing hard to get.
2. I incorrectly interpreted her nudity as forwardness.
3. She was not interested in me sexually, just trying to prevent embarrassment.
4. She just wanted to see how I would react.

Analysis of Options

1. There is no evidence of this. Aside from the obvious nudity, there was no attempt at flirting or mixed messages involved. Try again.
2. This is the best answer. I've come to the conclusion that most Europeans view nudity in public as a matter of course; it is done for convenience and nothing more. It's more convenient to bathe at the beach without tops or bottoms that leave tan lines or cause chaffing; it's more convenient to change in front of people instead of making a heroic effort at securing some privacy. In the U.S., the human body is considered dirty and should be hidden except in the most intimate of relationships. We simply had different perceptions of the meaning of nudity.
3. It was very kind of her to lend me her towel, but there is more going on here than her kindness. Embarrassing herself to save me embarrassment makes no sense. Choose again.
4. Her casual demeanor would indicate that her actions were normal and not part of an experiment. This answer is unlikely.

24

One of my very best friends to this day is a kid whose name is Bunty. His parents were born and raised in India and moved to Connecticut, where I grew up, just after Bunty was born. Bunty basically grew up as an American and didn't pay much attention to the Indian beliefs that his parents held.

Bunty and I became friends through Little League Baseball at the age of 9. He would come over to my house all the time, but we never went to his house. When we were 11, he finally invited me over for dinner after our baseball game. I had never been inside a home that wasn't occupied by Caucasians, so this was a new experience for me. I distinctly remember the scent that tickled my nose as we walked through the door, and I continue to smell it every time I enter their home.

We took off our muddy spikes, and changed into clean clothes after taking showers. I put on my sneakers and headed for the dining room to eat dinner. As we were in the middle of eating a tasty Indian dish, I heard Bunty's mom let out a very strange cry. I didn't know what was going on, but I knew it wasn't good. She excused herself and Bunty from the table and went into the other room to talk. I thought Bunty did something wrong, but it turned out it was me who made the mistake. Bunty returned to the table and told me that in India, disrespect is shown by those who wear shoes at dinner. I felt terrible. I had no idea of this belief, and since Bunty didn't pay much attention to their rules, he failed to tell me. His mom returned to the table a few minutes later and I gave a huge apology. I meant no disrespect to anyone, especially his parents, because at that age, disrespecting parents was probably the worst thing a child could do.

How could this situation have been avoided?

Options

1. Bunty's mom should not have overreacted.
2. I should have asked Bunty about their cultural rules.
3. I should have been more observant and noticed that no one else was wearing shoes.
4. This situation could not have been avoided.

Analysis of Options

1. This is the best answer. Bunty's mom, being the adult in the situation, should have understood that I was too young to have significant knowledge about other cultures. She should have been aware that I was from a different culture that followed different rules. In fact, she accepted my apology, recognizing that I wasn't aware of their beliefs. She also apologized to me for overreacting to the situation.
2. Knowing their cultural rules would have been helpful, but at age 11, not many kids are considerate enough or aware enough of cultural differences. Even if I had thought to ask, Bunty may not have thought of that particular rule to share with me. It's very difficult to explain one's cultural rules because we usually do not pay much attention to them until they are broken. This option is unlikely.

3. This action would also have been helpful. Learning to observe and match behavior is very helpful when communicating interculturally. And even at my young age, I could have paid more attention to what was going on around me. However, at that age I really was unaware of cultural differences, which is why I wasn't looking for any. There is a better answer.

4. Wrong answer. Choose again.

25

Rachell is Arabic and her friend, Lilian, is American. Lilian invited Rachell to a family dinner. Rachell had worn jeans and a sweater, nothing too formal. As Rachell got there she noticed everyone staring at her. It seemed as though everyone was dressed formally. Lilian had not mentioned to Rachell that it is their tradition to dress formally for dinner one time a week. Rachell felt very uncomfortable and pretended that her parents had paged her to come home because of a family emergency. Lilian was very upset because she knew the real reason Rachell left.

What should Rachell have done?

Options

1. Rachell should have done nothing differently. She felt uncomfortable.
2. Rachell should have stayed.
3. Rachell could have excused her appearance and explained the situation.
4. Rachell should have automatically dressed formally considering it was her first time meeting Lilian's family.

Analysis of Options

1. Rachell had every right to leave. She should not be made to feel uncomfortable. However, her actions are only going to cause discomfort later. There is a better answer.
2. Rachell showed disrespect by leaving, although Lilian showed disrespect to Rachell by not letting her know. Adapting to the situation would be better.
3. This is the best answer. They would have understood Rachell's situation if she had been polite and explained the situation. Unfortunately, in situations like these people often do not explain why they are behaving the way they are. They usually just avoid the situation and even end the relationship instead of actually talking about it. Explaining her appearance would have made everyone comfortable, and they all could have enjoyed the rest of their evening.
4. Rachell had no idea that she should have been dressed formally. If she had done so, and the situation was reversed, Rachell would have felt uncomfortable.

26

Through my job at a drug store I have met many different types of people from other countries who speak English as a second language. I even work with someone from the Middle East who speaks three languages. Although different cultures are very interesting to learn from for me, there have been a few incidents that I would rather not experience again.

I remember it was on a Saturday or Sunday and it was not really busy in the store. Now I work at the end of a long counter, which is filled with watches, beepers, sports cards, and other stuff, and I was working on an invoice of processed photos. While I was working on it I looked up and noticed a nicely dressed pair of Middle Eastern individuals strolling over to the end of the counter to look at the watches. I overheard some accents and thought I would make eye contact to see if they needed any assistance. I received no response right away and stayed in front of my register finishing my work.

Before I finished I heard a couple of whistles. I ignored them at first because I didn't think they were directing the noise toward me. I looked over in their direction when I heard the noise a second time to find out if they needed help. I walked over to the end of the counter and asked them if they were whistling at me. The men spoke very little English, but they said "yea" and inside I was really burning red. I told them in no uncertain terms that they should not whistle at me to get help or for any reason and that it was rude. I showed them their choices of watches and soon they left. I was glad that the two men didn't get offended at my tone also.

What happened here?

Options
1. The two men might have been arrogant fellows who expected and demanded attention by treating people like dogs.
2. The men were very patient and were just whistling tunes while they looked at watches and waited for their wives to finish shopping.
3. The two men have recently come to America and have few ways of communicating to Americans, so they tried to whistle as a gesture of help. This is most likely due to their effort and interests.

Analysis of Options
1. This is a possibility. However, since they are obviously from another culture, it is more likely that there is another reason. Choose again.
2. This is incorrect. The men indicated that they were whistling at me.
3. This is the best answer. The men probably did not realize that whistling in that manner is considered rude. Furthermore, since they could not speak English very well, they probably used a lot of nonverbal communication, such as whistling, to substitute for their words. It is fortunate that the men took my advice and did not start a conflict.

27

My friend Woody and I had just met in a psychology class. We exchanged phone numbers so we could get started on a psychology project that was due in a month. We had met many times at the coffee shop, worked on the project and made an outline of the final papers. All we had left to do was the final draft of the papers. However, this project required a computer to do the final step of the project. Woody suggested that we work on the final step of the project at my house, because I was the only one who had a computer. Strongly agreeing with what Woody had planned out, we decided to work on the final papers the next day and get the whole project completed.

The following day Woody arrived at my house at 1 P.M., which was the time that both of us had agreed on. When I opened the door, Woody just walked right on in and sat on the couch. I was very upset by this because Woody had not taken off his shoes. I just kept quiet, for I knew this was the last time Woody and I would have to meet to work on a class project. While we were putting the final papers together, I kind of gave Woody's shoes a dirty look. Even though I didn't want to make a big fuss, I know he saw my dirty look.

How would you help to explain Phu's reaction?

Options

1. Phu had just vacuumed the house and didn't want any dirt to trail into the house.
2. Phu had not asked Woody to take off his shoes, so Woody felt it wasn't a big concern.
3. Taking off your shoes at Phu's house is part of his culture. It is a custom that has been passed on to generations in his family and people.
4. Woody was so excited to get started on finishing the final paper that it didn't even occur to him to take off his shoes.
5. Walking all the way to Phu's house made Woody's legs tired and he needed to rest.

Analysis of Options

1. This would not be a logical choice; there is nothing mentioned of Phu's vacuuming his house. You are not reading the incident carefully.
2. This is a possibility. However, it doesn't explain Phu's displeasure.
3. This is the correct choice, because it is a matter of common respect and of being aware of others, especially when someone looks displeased, as Phu did. When you are in someone else's house, you are in a new culture. It doesn't seem that Woody was aware of it.
4. Nothing in this incident tells us that Woody is hyped up about getting started on the final step of the project. You must reread the incident again.
5. Nothing was discussed about Woody walking to Phu's house. Illogical choice. Please try again.

28

My mom worked for a Chinese lady in a Hallmark store for about five years. She and my mother became good friends. My mom taught her many customs that were practiced in the United States that were foreign to her. One time her family and my mom and I went out to eat at a semi nice restaurant. After dinner when we were waiting for the check Sue let out a very loud burp. I was in shock and started to laugh a little. My mom stopped me and I was in shock since my mom always yells at my brother for burping out loud.

How should I interpret this situation?

Options

1. All Chinese people are rude.
2. She has no manners and needs to get some.
3. In the Chinese culture it is a custom to burp after a meal because it is a compliment meaning it was good food.
4. She may have been drinking carbonated drinks and had bad gas.

Analysis of Options

1. This is an ethnocentric attitude and a stereotype. There is a better explanation.
2. It may be true that she is unaware of some U.S. taboos. However, that does not explain my mother's reaction. Choose again.
3. This woman was acting in a manner that was appropriate in her culture. My mother reacted the way she did because she was respectful of her customs, just as her friend was willing to learn many U.S. customs. My mother was showing a culturally relativistic response. It was acceptable for this woman to burp because it was her custom, but not acceptable for my brother to burp because it is not our custom.
4. This is always a possibility, but there is a better answer.

29

I was invited to my friend's house for dinner with her family. Because my friend is Hindi and I am Mexican, we have different customs. I had only been over to her house just a few times, and those few times her parents were either doing yard work or they were not home. When I arrived for dinner there was a pile of shoes at the entrance. I did not know whether to take off my shoes or not. I did not know what it meant, and I had never done it in the past, so why should I? I figured I would only make myself feel uncomfortable. As I approached the living room I was looked at very strangely.

What should I have done?

Options

1. I should have done nothing differently. I am not from their culture and should not be expected to know their ways.
2. Since the carpet was off-white, I should have checked my shoes for dirt.
3. Even though my friend did not tell me to take off my shoes, I should have done it out of respect to her family.
4. I should have asked if I should take off my shoes.

Analysis of Options

1. Doing nothing would still make everyone uncomfortable. Adapting to the situation would be a better tactic.
2. Checking shoes for dirt may still not make them clean. The issue here goes far beyond off-white carpet. Choose again.
3. This is the best answer. The significance of removing shoes varies from culture to culture. In the Hindi culture, it is not only an issue of cleanliness but also of respect. If my friend had asked me to take off my shoes in front of her parents it would have been as if she were pressuring me to show some respect.
4. While this would be better than not taking my shoes off at all, it is still a culturally ignorant choice. There is a better answer.

30

Ha, a Vietnamese man, and I work for the same company. Frequently we are required to interact in order to close transactions. The end of the month is always a very stressful time. Once that time passes, everyone is less on edge. It was at the beginning of one month when this incident occurred. Ha and I were working together along with his assistant when suddenly Ha began speaking in a very loud, high pitched fashion. I could not understand the words since he spoke in his native tongue. His assistant, also Vietnamese, reacted quickly to his directive with her eyes cast low without saying a word. Stunned at what I assumed was harsh treatment I quickly came to her defense. When confronted, Ha acted as though he had done nothing wrong and could not understand why I was upset. I left quietly, unsure how to conduct myself in future interactions.

How could you explain this incident?

Options

1. Ha was yelling at his assistant because he thought she was a stupid woman.
2. Ha was stressed out because he was frantically trying to close the transaction and his assistant and I were twiddling our thumbs.
3. In the Vietnamese language the inflection and pitch could often sound harsh to someone who is unfamiliar with Vietnamese linguistics.
4. Ha was speaking loudly because I am hard of hearing.

Analysis of Options

1. This is not a correct response since Ha expressed his confusion at my concern over his tone and expression.
2. Although this could be possible, it was the beginning of the month, which is typically a slower time.
3. This is the correct response. It is typical in the Vietnamese language to speak in loud and high-pitched tones. This does not, however, mean that Ha was angry or upset with any person.
4. There was no mention of any hearing impairment. Choose again.

31

This incident took place in New York City in 1979. The first time I went to the supermarket in this country I was walking down one aisle and a quite attractive girl was coming towards me from the opposite direction. When our eyes met she smiled, the most exquisite smile I have seen. My Mediterranean culture showed through my thoughts, "Come to my room, I'm no longer deceased," (Monty Python), etc. So I asked her, "What is your name?" She ignored me and went her way. Unfortunately, I insisted, because I thought she did not hear me. I touched her shoulder and asked again. At this point, she embarrassed me by shouting a few four-letter words. I was left completely shocked, speechless, and offended.

Why did this happen?

Options

1. The girl wanted to go out with me but she wanted to play tough.
2. I should have told her my name first.
3. Touching is inappropriate and furthermore she was scared.
4. The smiling of a woman to a man does not have a sexual connotation in the U.S.

Analysis of Options

1. This is very unlikely because she would have acknowledged my pass to her in the beginning. Instead she ignored me completely.
2. Since she ignored me I do not think that first telling her my name would make a difference.
3. This really makes sense since the incident took place in New York where people are watchful and wary.
4. This is a viable answer as well considering that smiling in this country is a form of civility and politeness, whereas in Greece (where I am from) a smile is an invitation.

32

Gina is from "back East" and works in Salt Lake City as a draftsman. At the time of this incident, her company was one of the biggest computer companies. She was the first and only woman in the department. She wanted to do well so she was working at what she considered to be an average steady pace. After a while, a couple of the gentlemen that she got to know told her to slow down because she was making them look bad. Gina did not know what to do. She wanted to get along with her coworkers, yet she wanted to do a good job and make an impression on her boss.

How should Gina respond to this situation?

Options

1. Should she tell them that this is her normal pace and continue to work fast?
2. Should she assume that they don't like the fact a woman is working with them and they are just trying to get her fired?
3. Should she go to the boss and tell him what they said?
4. Should she realize that she is from a different part of the country and people here might have a different meaning of time?

Analysis of Options

1. While this may be true, Gina could easily offend her coworkers by implying that they are slow. Choose again.
2. This could be a possibility, especially considering she is the first woman to work there. However, assuming the worst about their actions will not help communication to run smoothly. Gina should look for another explanation.
3. Definitely not. Try again.
4. This is a very good possibility. Different cultures have different perceptions of time and efficiency. While some focus on accomplishing tasks, others focus on relationships. Some prefer a fast pace whereas others prefer a more relaxed pace. Gina may not have had the same time orientation as her coworkers. Trying to adapt to their time orientation will not only make things easier for Gina but will also give her coworkers the sense that she is one of them.

33

One Friday night, Ferguson and I planned to attend this get-together at Mary Anne's house. Ferguson and I took our time getting ready. The party was arranged to begin at about 6:00 P.M. We left the house around 6:30. At about 7:00 P.M., we arrived. I thought we were arriving just in time. Mary Anne was shocked to see us. As she opened the door, she seemed welcoming. "Hi, Rosiella, I thought you weren't going to make it." As we entered the room everyone else was watching a movie. So we decided to join the group. At about 9:00, my stomach started growling. "Mary Anne, do you know what time we are having dinner?" She told me that everyone already ate. I was shocked at her response, but after a few seconds of hesitation she said, "but, I'll get you guys some anyway." I noticed an annoyed tone and asked Ferguson why she was upset. Ferguson had no idea either because he thought that she was just going to serve dinner late.

Why did Mary Anne react the way she did?

Options

1. She was too busy watching the movie and did not want to be interrupted.
2. She thought Rosiella was being rude by asking her host what time dinner will be.
3. She was worried about Rosiella and Ferguson because she thought they got into some kind of accident on the way to the party.
4. She was upset that Rosiella and Ferguson did not have the courtesy to be punctual.

Analysis of Options

1. Although she was interested in the movie, Mary Anne, as the hostess, was probably concerned more with concentrating on entertaining her guests. Try another option.
2. This is a possible response, but an incorrect one, because this wasn't the underlying reason why Mary Anne was upset. It might have made her more angry, but it did not cause the initial reaction.
3. This is an incorrect choice because Mary Anne's reaction would be more of relief than annoyance if this were true.
4. This is the best choice. Rosiella and Ferguson, who are Filipinos, are used to arriving late. In Tagalog slang it's called "pinoy time." As Filipinos, they thought it was correct to arrive late. On the other hand, Mary Anne expected everyone to be there at 6:00. At that time she would conclude that the guests who were not there would not show up.

34

One late afternoon I rushed into the local supermarket to pick up some items for dinner and lunch items for my children's lunch the next day. As I entered the store, I was shocked to see the lines. They were incredibly long. It wasn't even a holiday season. So, I rushed through the store, throwing items into the cart. I wanted to get in line as soon as possible, because I knew it would be a bit of a wait. I pushed my cart into line, and three or four other carts lined up behind me quickly. As I stood there, I saw a magazine cover that caught my eye. Since I often look at magazines while in line, I went up and grabbed the magazine off the rack. I was gone for less than 10 seconds. As I returned to my cart, I was horrified to see that an Asian woman had taken my cart out of line and taken my place. I approached her and asked what was going on. She either ignored me or didn't understand me. The people who had gotten in line behind me were not too pleased with this woman either. She turned her back to me and I moved her cart and took my rightful place back in line. She turned back, faced me, shrugged her shoulders and went on her way to another line.

What should I have done?

Options

1. I behaved correctly. My cart was in line, holding my place.
2. I should have allowed her to stay in line and say nothing.
3. I should have questioned her, and when she responded, got in the back of the line.
4. I should have called the manager of the store to settle the situation.

Analysis of Options

1. I don't think this was the correct way to respond since I am unfamiliar with the customs of this woman. She may have been behaving in a manner appropriate to her culture, and I simply made her feel uncomfortable. On the other hand, this behavior probably helped her to learn the rules for this situation.
2. This is probably the way I should have handled the situation. If I had not been in a hurry, I would have probably reacted this way. With so much diversity around us, it is much easier to assume that someone is following different cultural rules than to get stressed out over differences.
3. This option is not a good choice either, since the woman either did not speak English or chose to ignore me.
4. This option would probably not have been successful either. If the woman could not understand me, I'm sure she would not have been able to communicate with the manager either. It also would have wasted more of my time.

35

A few years ago I was working at the Fairmont Hotel in downtown San Jose. I was a senior member in the banquet department. We had the capability to serve up to two thousand people. With such large parties a large staff was also needed. I was in the definite minority, being born and raised in the Bay Area. Most of the staff was of Persian or Hispanic descent. This made communication a challenge on a daily basis. One incident I remember occurred between an older Persian waiter and myself. He was telling me a story and as he was talking to me in his broken English he kept getting closer; his face was less than a foot from mine. I felt he was invading my personal space and this made me uncomfortable. I backed up to increase the space between us, and as I did this he stopped talking, gave me a dirty look, and walked away.

Later that evening I told another Persian waiter about the incident. He told me that what I did was considered rude and disrespectful. As I was backing away my action was perceived as I wasn't interested in or didn't care about what this man had to say.

What should I have done?

Options

1. I should have done nothing, letting him finish his story.
2. I should have offered him a breath mint.
3. I should have tried to explain that he didn't have to be right in my face for me to listen to his story.
4. What I did was the right thing to do.

Analysis of Options

1. By doing nothing this would have been accommodating to his culture's way of communication. However, I would have still been uncomfortable. I think there is a better way.
2. Offering him a breath mint I'm sure would have been viewed as rude. This is not the best answer.
3. Trying to explain to him that he was invading my personal space would be the best thing to do. It might, however, not be the easiest thing to explain. After we reached a compromise we would both be happy with the outcome and be able to better communicate in the future. This is the best answer.
4. Obviously this was not the right thing to do. He felt I was rude and I didn't get to hear the end of the story. This is not the best answer.

36

After spending a semester with unbearable roommates, I moved to another room on the other side of the dorm. My new roommates seemed to be quite normal. Now I would be able to be comfortable and have fewer distractions to my studying. After a week or so, I began to get to know my roommates pretty well. We had a lot in common. We liked the same kind of music, the same kind of movies, and the same study schedules. One day while I was watching television, my roommate, Anatoa, from Tonga, decided to watch with me. She sat down very close to me. I was very uncomfortable. Then, while commenting on an aspect of the television show, she would touch my arm. Because I was so uncomfortable I would scoot away a little. She did not understand why it made me uncomfortable, and she did not stop.

Why was I so uncomfortable?

Options

1. I did not approve of Anatoa's advances.
2. I did not like it when people talked while I was watching television.
3. Anatoa invaded my personal space.
4. It was my turn to sit on the couch and I did not want to share.

Analysis of Options

1. Though she was sitting very close and she was touching my arm, it is not very likely that she was coming on to me. Choose another answer.
2. The talking did not upset me. Many people do not like talking while watching television, but this was not the problem in this case. Choose another answer.
3. My idea of personal space has been very ingrained into my head since I was very young. Anatoa, being from Tonga, has been raised in a very different environment. Everyone is very close and touching is very normal. I needed to realize that was how she was raised. Then I would be able to deal with the situation.
4. This is a ridiculous idea. Who would set couch-sitting time? Choose another answer.

37

Like every morning when I arrive at work, I will greet each of the manufacturing line employees before I begin my day. The majority of the crew is from Chinese and Vietnamese descent. Since I manage some of the people, I strive to get to know them and their feelings about their jobs. From time to time, I attempt to learn the greeting customs of their origins to create a feeling of comfort and belonging among them. I usually approach them with either a simple "Hello!" or "Good Morning," or "How are you?" Once in a while, I would place my hand on their shoulder or gently pat them on the back as I greet them. This went on for many months without incident.

However, early one morning, as I said my "hello's" to the employees, Fanny, a co-worker of Chinese origin, ignored my greeting and pat on the shoulder. She continued her work as if I was not there. Even though I did not manage her line, I thought this was rather odd. I tried to greet her again, and she told me not to talk to her ever again. I asked her what was wrong and she refused to tell me. I felt she was being rude. This bewildered me and I wondered what I had done to upset her.

What was the most likely reason for Fanny's reaction?

Options

1. Fanny was having a bad morning and did not want to be bothered that particular day.
2. I violated a rather complex system of power structure that exists in the Chinese culture without knowing about it.
3. Fanny was annoyed and uncomfortable by the touching part of my greeting.
4. There was a prior problem between Fanny and I that I did not know about.

Analysis of Options

1. This scenario is possible. However, she indicated that she did not want to speak to me ever again. If she was having a bad day, she could have told me. In the Chinese culture, it is important to be blunt about how you are feeling, even if it slightly offends the other person. So I would have at least been made aware that she was having a bad morning.
2. Individuals from the Chinese culture want to maintain a boss/co-worker relationship without friendship. Nevertheless, individuals from Asian countries do not like being singled out. Since we are working in an American environment, it would not be suitable for her to argue with any of the management.
3. This is the best answer. Many Asian cultures restrict any form of touching, even when greeting. Touching is especially limited between men and women. This is to respect their marriages or parents. In the Chinese culture, they slightly bow their heads in greeting each other. Even though the culture is quite tolerant of other customs infringing upon their own, individuals will erupt if they have had enough. I should have been more aware of this by asking more questions and understanding her point of view. The cross-cultural experience accepts this lashing out of frustration. It is not abnormal to encounter this behavior, especially between two very different cultures.
4. There is no evidence that there was a problem between Fanny and I. Please choose again.

38

I am a copy operator at Office Max and I work in the store's business center. Aside from running the Xerox machines, I take orders for business cards that we offer customers through a catalog. One evening an older gentleman, who seemed to be from Afghanistan, came up to my counter and wanted to place an order for some cards. As I was filling out his order form I felt him staring at me. This was making me slightly uncomfortable. I lowered my head so it was only a few inches away from the form and started writing rather quickly. Then he leaned over the counter, to my level, and we were practically nose to nose. I moved a little to the right and he followed me. By the time I had finished filling out the order form we were not in the spot that we first started out at. We had moved halfway across the counter.

What happened?

Options

1. This customer was making a pass at me.
2. He was trying to make me nervous and uncomfortable on purpose.
3. There are differences in the use of personal space from culture to culture. In some cultures it is appropriate to stand so close to someone that you can smell them.
4. The customer was watching me closely to make sure I didn't make any mistakes on the order form.

Analysis of Options

1. I was feeling paranoid. I was confronted with different behavior that I was not familiar with. There is a better answer.
2. I don't like to be undermined and I am confronted with a lot of customers that yell at me for no reason, particularly because of my age. However, assuming this was the case would only make the situation hostile. Choose again.
3. In Arab culture the personal space zone is a lot closer than the American culture. In fact, in American culture people normally stand approximately 4 feet apart to conduct business, whereas in Arab cultures there is no concept of personal space.
4. Most customers are very picky and do watch me very closely to make sure I don't mess up their business card orders. However, this was a little extreme. There is a more likely explanation.

39

In Mrs. Johnson's sixth grade math class, one of her best students, Thanh, is a recent immigrant from Vietnam. Living in the United States for almost a year now, Thanh has excelled academically throughout all of her classes. One day during her math class, Mrs. Johnson asked Thanh to come up to the front of the class to solve a math problem. Thanh came up to the front of the class without any hesitation and quickly solved the problem. She then quickly got back to her seat. During the whole time she never once looked at her teacher even when her teacher was directing a question at her. Mrs. Johnson didn't know why and thought Thanh was probably having a bad day so she didn't say anything. This was the first and not the last incident to follow. One day during recess, Mrs. Johnson was walking past the quad and saw Thanh. Mrs. Johnson asked Thanh how she was doing in all of her classes. Thanh, with her head down, told her she was doing great and then continued to read her book. Mrs. Johnson wondered why Thanh never looked directly at her when she was talking.

How would you explain Thanh's behavior to Mrs. Johnson?

Options

1. Thanh didn't like her teacher so she was being disrespectful to Mrs. Johnson.
2. Thanh was raised to be very shy.
3. Thanh was annoyed for being picked on to solve problems.
4. Thanh was being respectful to her elders so she would never look directly at her teacher while being talked to.

Analysis of Options

1. This does not seem possible because Mrs. Johnson was not picking on Thanh. Mrs. Johnson was merely trying to show the class that if Thanh can do it, then any of them can solve the problem.
2. This is possible because Asian children have been raised to be discrete in public but up to a certain point. There is a more likely answer.
3. This does not seem likely because Thanh was not the only student to be called on by Mrs. Johnson.
4. This is definitely the best response. In most Asian countries, children have been raised to show respect to their elders at all times. When a child is confronted by his or her teacher, he or she bows the head down to show respect. Asian children have been raised to never look directly at their elders because it represents defiance. Unlike the Asian cultures, American culture perceives not looking at someone when they are talking to be very disrespectful. Mrs. Johnson in turn thought Thanh was not paying attention to her, but on the contrary, Thanh was just showing respect to her teacher.

Comments

Nonverbal communication is any form of communication without the use of words. Consequently, this means there are literally endless methods to express oneself nonverbally. Nonverbal communication can be very ambiguous and is extremely culture bound, as we can see in the previous incidents. People often follow nonverbal rules for communication unconsciously. That is, we don't really stop to think about how we're communicating or even what we're expecting from others. However, nonverbal communication is also very powerful, so when we don't receive the nonverbal messages we're comfortable with and expecting, we usually react with a negative perception of the offending person or situation.

There are many different ways to express oneself nonverbally. Two of the most common types are *kinesics* and *proxemics*. Kinesics refers to the nonverbal messages we send with our bodies. This includes facial expression, eye contact, gestures, posture, paralanguage, appearance, and others. Proxemics refers to the way we use the space around us. This includes distance, territory, architecture, time, and others. A few of these aspects of nonverbal communication are explained in detail below.

Kinesics

Gestures

Gestures are motions of the body, usually the hands, that have specific communication value. In the U.S. we wave to say hello or goodbye and we use the "thumbs-up" to indicate that things are going well. However, gestures are incredibly culture bound, and therefore may have different meanings from culture to culture. For example, the thumbs-up is a vulgar gesture in Iran and the OK sign (touching index finger to thumb) is vulgar just about everywhere else. Thus, it becomes incredibly easy to offend someone from another culture without even being aware of it.

Eye Behavior

Eye behavior refers to eye contact and length of gaze. Eye contact sends messages of respect, involvement, or dominance. However, as with all nonverbal communication, cultural rules will differ. So different types of behaviors may indicate respect, involvement, or dominance. For instance, most Western cultures prefer direct eye contact as a symbol of respect. It shows one is paying attention and is involved in the conversation. However, many Eastern cultures prefer just the opposite. Avoiding eye contact may mean respect and involvement. So in these cases direct eye contact would appear rude, pushy, and even arrogant. Clearly, differences in eye behavior can cause misunderstandings, as we can see in incident 39.

Paralanguage

Even the use of our voices is considered nonverbal communication. This means our tone of voice, pitch, rate, volume, pauses, rhythm, and even use of silence communicates a message. Of course, the perceptions of the appropriate way to use one's voice differ from culture to culture. A loud, sharp tone may indicate anger, excitement, involvement, emotion, or may just be considered normal depending upon the culture. This explains the misinterpretation that occurred in incident 30. Ignorance of paralinguistic rules leads us quickly to miscommunication.

Touch

Some people are particularly sensitive to specific nonverbal behaviors. Touch is one aspect of nonverbal communication for which people have very strict rules. Because of this, we become incredibly uncomfortable when those rules are violated. Unfortunately, this is also another area where cultural rules will differ. Thus, when communicating interculturally, we will have to deal with differing perceptions of touch. According to Hall (1959) some cultures tend to be *contact cultures*. In contact cultures people touch more, stand closer together, speak face-to-face, engage in direct eye contact, and use louder volume. Southern American, Southern European, Arabic, and Polynesian cultures tend to be contact cultures. In *noncontact cultures* people tend to touch less, stand farther apart, use less direct eye contact, and use softer volume. United States, Northern European, and Asian cultures tend to be noncontact cultures. So you can see how easily the rules for touch can be violated. A noncontact person may even be horrified at the fact that someone is touching him or her, whereas a contact person may be insulted if you don't touch him or her. These differences are illustrated in incidents 36 and 37.

Proxemics

Distance

Whereas touch is one way to communicate with our bodies, distance is one way to communicate with our use of space. As you can see in the previous discussion above, touch and distance are intricately connected. Hall's research indicates that people in the United States have specific preferences for the distances kept in various contexts. In his research, he describes four distances: intimate, personal, social, and public. Intimate distance, with people we are closest to, is within 18 inches. Personal distance, in casual conversations, is between 18 inches and 4 feet. Social distance, usually business interactions, is 4 feet to 7 feet. Finally, public distance, occurring in the context of speeches as opposed to interaction, is usually over 12 feet. While these distances make sense for most people in the U.S., the same is not true in other cultures. Many contact cultures cannot even imagine the concept of having one's own personal "space bubble" around them. Consequently, people from different cultures will find they are constantly trying to adjust "their space." Argyle and Dean's (1965) concept of *affiliative conflict theory of intimacy* applies here. This theory explains that any change in an intimacy indicator (touch, distance, eye contact, etc.) by one individual will elicit a compensatory change in the other individual. In terms of distance, this means people will "do the dance." If one person prefers a closer distance while the other prefers a farther one, each will continue to try to adjust the space between them to a point that feels most comfortable. Since what is most comfortable may be drastically different for each person, a type of dance tends to occur. This consequence is described in incident 35. Once the dance begins, both people tend to misinterpret each other's actions and become offended.

Time Orientation

Most students coping with the diversity of the United States have experienced the conflict of different time orientations. Some cultures are what Hall (1959) labels as *monochronic*. A *monochronic time orientation* is one where people see time as a specific duration. For example, class begins promptly at 1:30 and ends by 3:00. In a monochronic culture, a later start or completion time is unacceptable, and students would probably leave the classroom with scowls on their faces! Many people in monochronic cultures have datebooks in which they schedule every half-hour of their day from 7 A.M. to 7 P.M. Time is money. Time can be wasted. Time is ticking. Such is the monochronic perception of time. However, a *polychronic time orientation* is very different. Polychronic cultures see time as a sequence of events. A student will go to class after lunch, and go to the library after class, and meet friends for dinner when he is done at the library. One event follows another. There is no strict adherence to the clock.

This time orientation tends to run on a *continuum*, with some cultures being extremely polychronic, others being extremely monochronic, and yet still others falling in between. Some cultures vary their time orientation with the context. For example, one may go by the clock at work and be more relaxed when it comes to social gatherings.

Since the U.S. consists of such a diversity of cultures, this conflict in time orientation often occurs right here at home. Hence the terms Pinoy Time, Hawaiian Time, Colored People's Time (CPT), etc. Unfortunately, this knowledge is often forgotten when we interact with others, as in incident 33. Since monochronic cultures consider every minute valuable, lateness is interpreted negatively. To a monochronic person, lateness indicates a lack of respect, a power struggle, or irresponsibility. Any of these interpretations can cause a monochronic person to feel unappreciated or not valued. However, a polychronic person simply does not follow the clock; he or she would arrive "when I get there." Hence a late arrival. In fact, many polychronic cultures count on a late arrival, so an invitation for dinner at 6 P.M. could actually mean 7:30 P.M., 9 P.M., or 10 P.M. Arriving at 6 P.M. would actually be too early and would cause embarrassment.

Consequences

Fundamental attribution error and autistic hostility rear their ugly heads again here with nonverbal communication. As you recall, *fundamental attribution error* is when we make negative judgments about people because they did not follow *our* cultural rules without understanding *their* cultural rules. This often leads to *autistic hostility*, which is unexpressed anger resulting from intercultural misunderstanding. So in incident 33, we have Mary Anne (monochronic) interpreting her guest's lateness as disrespectful toward her and her efforts to provide a pleasant dinner on time. Whereas her guests (polychronic) simply did not feel the rush to arrive exactly at 6:00 P.M. In incident 35 we have the waiter so offended by the increase in distance that he abruptly ends the conversation. The difficulty in communication lies in the fact that people do not discuss these problems. They usually simply leave the interaction angry and offended. If Mary Anne had expressed her anger, or if the guests had expressed their confusion, this problem would have been swiftly resolved.

Nonverbal Communication Exercises

Exercise 1. Nonverbal Observation Activity

Following the directions your instructor gives you, observe and record your partners' reactions using the following criteria:

- general body movements

    person one: _____

    person two: _____

- skin tone (flushed, sweaty, etc.)

    person one: _____

    person two: _____

- position and posture

    person one: _____

    person two: _____

- manipulators (fidgeting, winding hair, cleaning nails, etc.)

    person one: _____

    person two: _____

- distance

    person one: _____

    person two: _____

- hesitations

    person one: _____

    person two: _____

- talk-time

    person one: _____

    person two: _____

- voice (speed, volume)

    person one: _____

    person two: _____

- object adapters

    person one: _____

    person two: _____

Following the directions your instructor gives you, observe and record your partners' reactions using the following criteria:

- general body movements

  person one: _____

  person two: _____

- skin tone (flushed, sweaty, etc.)

  person one: _____

  person two: _____

- position and posture

  person one: _____

  person two: _____

- manipulators (fidgeting, winding hair, cleaning nails, etc.)

  person one: _____

  person two: _____

- distance

  person one: _____

  person two: _____

- hesitations

  person one: _____

  person two: _____

- talk-time

  person one: _____

  person two: _____

- voice (speed, volume)

  person one: _____

  person two: _____

- object adapters

  person one: _____

  person two: _____

Exercise 2. Personal Assessment Questions

A.   Observe and record your nonverbal communication for three days. What do you find you do most often?

_____

_____

_____

_____

B.   Observe the nonverbal communication of other people with whom you interact. Describe the behaviors that are difficult to interpret. _____

_____

_____

_____

_____

C.   Pair up with a partner. One person should read the following passage, using his or her voice to express the following emotions: passion, anger, love, embarrassment, and confidence. The other person should try to guess the emotion, explaining why he or she came to that conclusion. Switch roles and repeat the process.

Passage: Hush little baby don't say a word
              Momma's going to buy you a mocking bird
              If that mocking bird don't sing,
              Momma's going to buy you a diamond ring
              If that diamond ring is brass
              Momma's going to buy you a looking glass
              If that looking glass gets broke
              Momma's going to buy you a billy goat
              If that billy goat runs away
              Momma's going to buy you another today.

Exercise 3. Cultural Partner Question

Discuss with your partner the differences in nonverbal communication between his or her original culture and the culture you are both experiencing now. Did your partner experience any misunderstandings because of these differences?

Chapter Three

Social Roles

40

Paul and Maria are juniors in college and have been going out with each other since their freshman year. Paul is from the United States and Maria is an exchange student from Mexico. Paul really wants Maria to move in with him but the apartment is too small for three people, and Paul's father has been living with him ever since he had a stroke. One day Paul called Maria on the phone excitedly saying, "You can move in. I'm going to place my father in a nursing home." Maria remained quiet, then hung up the phone.

Why did Maria react that way?

Options

1. Maria thinks Paul does not care about his father.
2. Maria does not really want to move in with Paul. It's not considered proper in her culture.
3. Maria thinks badly of nursing homes.
4. Maria thinks Paul should continue to take care of his dad.

Analysis of Options

1. This would be the best response. Mexican people are taught to look after their parents, especially if they are sick. Paul thinks a nursing home would be a great idea, but Maria looks at it differently. The elderly are to be honored and respected in Mexican culture whereas in American culture people are admired for being youthful. Hence, nursing homes that separate the elderly from the youthful are expected and natural in the United States, while in Mexico it is natural and expected to venerate the elderly in your family by giving them a place in your home.
2. This can also be a possibility because she was shocked Paul asked her to move in with him so soon. Due to the predominance of the Catholic religion in the Mexican culture, two unmarried people living together is believed to be wrong and immoral.
3. This response is unlikely because Maria could have discussed the quality of nursing homes with Paul.
4. While Maria probably does think Paul should continue to take care of his dad, this is not a likely reason for such a strong reaction. The larger issue in this incident is showing respect to his father. Choose again.

41

Richard, an African-American, and I, an international student from Japan, have been going out for 14 months. Since my family members live in Japan, I go back to Japan once a year to visit them. A month ago, I told Richard about my trip to Japan for the winter break, and asked him if he could give me a ride to the airport. He said, "yes," but seemed confused. A couple of weeks later, I told him that I made a reservation for a flight. He then seemed offended when I told him about it.

Why was Richard offended?

Options

1. He didn't want to give me a ride.
2. He missed me.
3. He was jealous about my trip.
4. He felt offended because I didn't invite him to come with me.

Analysis of Options

1. This is unlikely. He always tells me if something is wrong with him, and there was no force on him to agree to give me a ride.
2. This might have been a part of his feeling because we have been spending time together as much as possible since we started going out. However, this is not the best answer.
3. This is not the answer. Even though I was so excited about the trip, he understood that I hadn't seen my family for one year.
4. This is the best answer. Japanese are not so open to boyfriend-girlfriend relationships, and it is not common to invite a boyfriend or girlfriend to one's parents' house like it is in American culture. He must have thought that I didn't want to introduce him to my parents or I wasn't as serious about our relationship as he was.

42

Ann, a Mexican-American who was born and raised in the United States, was getting ready to meet her grandparents from Mexico for the first time. That same night she had her boyfriend over to introduce him to her grandparents. After they were introduced to each other they took a seat and Ann, without thinking about her grandparents, sat on her boyfriend's lap. Right away the grandparents stood up and moved to another room. Ann could not understand their behavior.

Why did Ann's grandparents react the way they did?

Options

1. The grandparents were shocked by Ann's behavior.
2. The grandparents felt offended by Ann's physical move.
3. The grandparents were upset because Ann was giving all the attention to her boyfriend.
4. The grandparents thought it was right for them to give Ann and her boyfriend time to be alone.

Analysis of Options

1. This is the best answer. Freedom to show affection is different among cultures. In some parts of Mexico it is not appropriate for a girl to sit on her boyfriend's lap. The grandparents were probably embarrassed and shocked to see Ann's behavior and left not knowing what to say. While many cultures, including Mexican culture, prefer close contact, there are often strict rules that apply to male/female relations. Touching in this way between a boyfriend and a girlfriend is considered promiscuous and unacceptable.
2. This is not the best answer. While Mexican culture is high contact, one is not expected to sit closely to another at all times, nor is one offended if someone moves farther away.
3. The story indicates that Ann sat on her boyfriend's lap, not that she ignored her grandparents. Choose again.
4. It is not likely that the grandparents would want Ann to spend time alone with her boyfriend. In fact, they would probably prefer to be chaperones. Please choose again.

43

I have been going out with my girlfriend for about one year. She was born and raised in a U.S. culture while I was born in Mexico and raised there until I was ten. I had met all of her rather large immediate family and had spent considerable time with them. I thought of them as good people and from what my girlfriend told me, they thought I was a cool guy and they liked having me around. When I would go to her house, the only unpleasant thing was her youngest sister. She came off as an extremely rude five-year-old. She threw fits constantly, hit people thinking this was funny, ignored direct instructions from her parents, fought loudly with her slightly older brother, and basically always got her way. Where I am from, children very rarely act like this because they are disciplined and taught to act in certain ways when there is company. My girlfriend simply said that she is the youngest so she was accustomed to babying and not to worry, "Soon she will be used to you and she will be nicer to you."

So sure enough, after a few more months little Chelsea started to be nicer and it was tolerable to be around her. One day, my girlfriend and I took Chelsea to the park and afterward we stopped at my house because I had some stuff to take care of. My sister was there and when Chelsea started to throw a tantrum, my sister looked at her with a face of disgust. I got up and told my sister in Spanish that she was a little spoiled so she was used to always getting her way. She and I started watching Chelsea and talking about how where we were from, kids are taught completely differently and her behavior would be looked upon as ill breeding. Within a few minutes, my girlfriend grabbed her sister by the hand and left my house.

Why did my girlfriend leave so abruptly with her sister?

Options

1. She thought that my sister and I should have talked about her sister's behavior in English rather than in Spanish.
2. My girlfriend's feelings were hurt because she noticed that we were looking at Chelsea and she caught the tone of our conversation.
3. She was running late on some errand and had no time to say good-bye.
4. My girlfriend doesn't like my sister and she gets mad when I speak with her in her presence.

Analysis of Options

1. Though this is a possible explanation, my girlfriend probably would not appreciate bad comments about her sister in English or any other language. This is not the best choice.
2. This is the most probable explanation. It hurt my girlfriend's feelings to hear my sister and I talk poorly about Chelsea. Even though she is aware of Chelsea's behavior, she still loves her sister very much and she did not think it was any of my business to make comments about her conduct or how she should be raised. However, since there is a much greater emphasis on discipline in my culture, my sister and I considered it normal to discuss children's behavior. Additionally, we did not perceive Chelsea to be deserving of respect since she was a child. One earns respect through age.
3. There was no mention of any errands in this incident to indicate that she could not say good-bye before she left. This is not the right explanation.
4. Though this may be the case, it was not mentioned in this incident. Therefore, it cannot be the right choice.

44

While attending Davis I became engaged to my husband, Pete. My parents were a bit upset at the time for several reasons. One reason was he was Swedish ("white" in my parents' eyes) and my family members were very traditional Mexicans. The second reason was my parents and my family had never even met Pete before. In our culture, courting is something that parents and family are well aware of. Perhaps this is why when I called to give them the good news they were not exactly thrilled. Naturally, my parents and my family were eager to meet this soon to be new member of their family. That following week we made arrangements to drive down to Bakersfield, CA. Upon arriving, I knew tensions would be high. Pete did his best to try and ease the tension by showing my entire family a great deal of respect. Unfortunately, this did not last long.

My mother and sisters were preparing a very traditional dinner. After a few minutes we were all summoned to the dining table. After we said grace we all began eating our food. We were well into our meal when my mom noticed that Pete was not eating. She asked, "Pete, why are you not eating? Maria told me you love Mexican food."

Pete replied, "I do Mrs. Garcia, but why is there no silverware, only a spoon?"

My mother then turned to me and said in Spanish, "If he is going to be a part of this family he should learn that some meals that we eat, we eat with tortillas and very little silverware. See, this is why it is difficult to date out of your own. People just do not understand even the smallest things about our culture!"

How could have this miscommunication and misunderstanding been resolved?

Options

1. I could have asked my mom ahead of time what she would be serving.
2. My mom could have prepared something else that we could eat with silverware and tortillas.
3. Pete could have asked me quietly for more silverware, such as a fork and knife.
4. Pete could have said he was sorry, but that he was not that great at eating with tortillas, and would like a full set of silverware.
5. Pete just should have tried eating with tortillas and not said anything.

Analysis of Options

1. By asking my mom what she would be serving, I could have briefed Pete that this meal is eaten with tortillas and very little silverware. This way he could have been prepared.
2. By asking my mom to prepare something different, she probably would have become offended because Pete is a guest in her home.
3. By Pete asking me for silverware, would have drawn more scrutiny to his character.
4. By Pete saying he was sorry probably would have been okay, but my family would have said he should have tried anyway.
5. If Pete had picked up a tortilla and the spoon and just started eating without saying anything, my family would have respected him for trying.

45

Sarah and John have been dating for over a period of one year. John attended Sarah's family gatherings and seemed to fit in just fine. Then one day, Sarah received a call from her aunt, Pamela, inviting her to travel with the family down to San Diego to visit other relatives. Sarah thought this would be a perfect opportunity for John to get to know the rest of the family. They packed up and drove to San Diego. It was a long, 8-hour drive in a cramped car. Upon arriving at the house, they were greeted very warmly by 20 or so people. There was much hugging and smiles being exchanged while John just stood there oddly out of place. Then Sarah's aunt shouted, "Please have a seat. Dinner will be served." John walked over to the table first since Sarah was still socializing. One by one, the men started sitting down around the table. John was expecting Sarah to sit down next to him but instead, an elderly male sat down in that chair. When John looked around the room for Sarah, she was nowhere to be found. He later heard her voice coming from the kitchen. Dinner was served and John fit in quite well, carrying conversations with all the relatives, but he thought it was quite odd that there were no females at the table. After dinner, Sarah came out of the kitchen and asked John if he liked the food being served. John nodded and walked off. Sarah was left standing there confused at his abrupt behavior.

Why did John ignore Sarah after dinner?

Options

1. John thought Sarah was mad at him and did not want to be anywhere near him.
2. John felt confused and abandoned when Sarah did not sit down next to him.
3. John likes to socialize with her relatives.
4. He did not like the strange food being served and felt Sarah should have forewarned him.

Analysis of Options

1. Not a good answer. Nowhere in the story did it indicate Sarah was mad at John. Please choose again.
2. This is the best answer. In certain parts of Vietnam, it is common for all the men to sit down together at a formal gathering while the women gather together in the kitchen or with their own table. John did not know why the table was full of men and all the women disappeared into the kitchen. He felt Sarah could have explained this to him before he sat down so that he didn't feel like she abandoned him.
3. This could be a possible answer since John did get along well with Sarah's relatives. But it still doesn't explain why he just walked off on Sarah so abruptly. There is a better explanation.
4. This is not the correct answer. John did not indicate at any time that he did not enjoy the food. In fact, he nodded yes when Sarah asked him if he liked it. Please select again.

46

Early in John and Lori's relationship, a barbecue/reunion was held at John's sister Janey's house. All the extended family would be there and everyone was excited.

As John drove up the driveway, you could see people hugging, laughing, and crying all at once. Soon they were both out of the car and into the house to enjoy the festivities. No sooner had they stepped foot in the door when all the men made a beeline toward the ice chest and the lawn chairs!

Meanwhile, the women migrated to the kitchen. Lori tagged along and was soon washing and drying with the rest of the women. Before you knew it, dinner was served.

No sooner had THAT announcement been made when a large, hungry herd of men stormed through the kitchen to the family room and planted themselves on the chairs, couches, and floors looking very hungry. When the men were all settled, the women went into action. Lori had never seen so many people doing so many things in so little space! Lori got lost in the shuffle when Janey handed her a plate and instructed her to serve John his dinner. As she began to do so, she watched as the others would stand near their man so as to attend to his every need. Feeling a bit embarrassed, Lori took John his plate and went to hide in the back of the kitchen. Later as everyone was cleaning up, some of the women looked annoyed at her and whispered in Spanish as they walked by her.

Later as John drove home, Lori told her tale and expressed her belief that his family members' ways were outdated and demeaning to women. John, who had a wonderful visit with his family, felt Lori was making a mountain out of a molehill and told her so. Then he dismissed her feelings and refused to discuss it any more.

What happened here?

Options

1. John's family was out to get Lori because she is not Hispanic. They felt that Lori wasn't good enough for John so they tried to make things as uncomfortable as they could.
2. Lori was angry that John paid no attention to her all day so she used the dinner mishap to start a fight.
3. Being independent in nature, Lori felt that the act of women serving men in such a fashion was a step backward for women.
4. Because of the differences between John and Lori's upbringing, what was perceived by Lori as subservient behavior is seen by John as a loving, respectful gesture.

Analysis of Options

1. John's family had treated Lori as a member of the family and as far as you can tell by the text, this was not a race issue. The only problem was Lori's apparent disrespect for John. Perhaps the reason for the whispers was that the other women were looking for a kind way to explain their customs.
2. This may seem like a solution, but what it really was the reaction to a perceived slight or injustice. Anger is generally not an answer, but a response. Lori's anger was probably born of her confusion.
3. Being of an independent nature does not a feminist make! Lack of knowledge contributed to Lori's feelings of embarrassment, not the roles each gender subsequently played.

4. This is the hidden problem here. Not realizing just how truly different their two cultures were, they neglected to discuss what might be expected of each other before they went to the party. Particularly, they each misinterpreted behaviors that demonstrated respect.

47

About seven years ago, I met a guy named Tony. He was an Italian who had recently moved from New Jersey to California to work for his uncle. He worked next door to my work and we would talk when we saw each other. He was very outgoing and bold. After a week of talking, he asked me out on a date. I accepted.

On the night of the date, he arrived a half-hour early. I wasn't quite ready, so I asked him to wait in the living room while I dressed. As I was dressing in my room, I could hear him in the living room yelling, "Get a move on, we got reservations!"

At dinner, in an expensive, quiet restaurant, he spoke very loudly across the table and addressed our waitress as "honey" and "toots." After dinner, he suggested we go back to my apartment. Being caught off guard, I agreed. When we got to my apartment, he plopped on the couch, removed his shoes, propped his feet on the coffee table, and talked about our next date. He thought it would be a good idea if for our second date, I made his favorite meal. He then began to dictate his Italian mother's best recipe for spaghetti and salad.

At the end of the evening, I decided that from then on I would avoid him at work. If he called I would tell him I'm involved with someone else, which is what I did two days later.

Why didn't I want to date him again?

Options

1. California women prefer to make dates with men after the first date.
2. When he removed his shoes after dinner at my apartment, I noticed he had horrible foot odor.
3. I felt he was too loud, rude, demanding, and impatient on this date. I wasn't used to such outspoken behavior.
4. He was trying too hard to impress me by taking me to an expensive restaurant when I knew where he worked and knew he didn't make much money.

Analysis of Options

1. There is no known rule on whether men or woman ask for the second date in California. This is false. Choose again.
2. This is partially true, but had he been nicer on the date, it could have been possibly overlooked, possibly.
3. This explanation was true. Italians tend to be contact cultures with large families creating lots of commotion and in order to be heard they must speak loudly. Italians also tend to be demonstrative in their gestures and expressions. Living on the East Coast added to Tony's personality. New Jersey is a congested, crowded area where survival is a high priority. East Coast residents tend to be less concerned with courtesy. Because of the different cultures and dense population in New Jersey, residents must be more aggressive for their needs.

   Californians differ because we have a more relaxed environment. We're considered "laid back." In California there is much emphasis on relaxing and creating more leisure time. We also concentrate highly on physical appearances and behaviors as indicators to who we are. I felt insulted and embarrassed by Tony's loud, demanding personality. My expectation of our date was a nice, quiet, romantic evening.

4. Choose again. His behaviors outweighed any monetary issues.

48

I was fifteen years old when I met my ex-boyfriend, Richard. He was born in Vietnam and came to the U.S. when he was eight years old. My family came from the Philippines, but my siblings and I were born and raised in America. We met through mutual friends and started to really get to know each other. He was 17 years old and a junior at a public school. I, on the other hand, was a sophomore at an all-girls private school.

We started dating and became sort of serious about each other. We got along well, and shared identical interests. However, our families were very different. He came from a strict family. For instance, his mom was altogether against him having a girlfriend. She thought that if he had a girlfriend it would take his time away from his studies and set a bad example for his younger sister. She said, "In Vietnam, there were arranged marriages and here girls his age are not wholesome enough." He wanted to avoid confrontation with her so he lied and said I was a "close friend" every time I called. I barely met her a year later because we were terrified of her finding out. He was about two years older, and he had to be home before me! His parents would wait up for him and nag him saying that it was not good to be out past ten o'clock. He would always lie about where he was. His mom would get irate if he used the phone after he got home in the evenings.

I, of course, hated it. I was not used to such an authoritarian lifestyle. My family is very lenient for a Filipino family. We were raised more with the typical American values all our lives. They never badgered us about where we were as much as his family did, and were happy with us just calling when we were going to go home, especially if it got pretty late. They did not mind us dating at that age and liked Rich a whole lot.

We used to argue about this because I always wanted more time to spend with him, but he would always HAVE to go home; even in the middle of a heated discussion! It was too hard for me to adjust and just accept the fact that his family can "never know." I know he meant well, but I just could not stand the lying and having to leave places early because he has to be home. I could not get to see much of him or converse with him on the phone. It put too much of a strain on our relationship. We were together for almost two years. I remember hoping that when he is at least 18 or out of high school things would change. They never did, and eventually we broke up. Honestly, it was hard because we broke up over circumstances and different cultural backgrounds.

How could we have resolved our differences?

Options

1. I should have accommodated to his culture and lifestyle.
2. Richard should have accommodated to me by being honest with his parents about our relationship.
3. We should have discussed our cultural identities and future plans.

Analysis of Options

1. I guess it would have worked out better if I understood where he was coming from and saw things from his perspective. I could have had a more open mind, but I guess I just got tired of accommodating my lifestyle to his. It was too unfair for me. This option did not work for us.
2. Instead of lying to his family all the time, he could have tried to rationalize with them and point out how sometimes they cannot control and monitor his actions twenty-four seven. We could have even talked to them

together and given them a chance to trust us. However, they probably would have considered this action disrespectful. Even if I did meet them, they probably would have tried to keep us apart and tell him that I was not good enough for him. They would not say it out of spite, but just because they thought girlfriends were a waste of time and I was another burden in his life.

3. This is probably the best option, although it still may not have kept us together. Both of us didn't understand how important these cultural traditions and ways of living were to each of us. Obviously, neither one of us was comfortable accommodating, but perhaps discussing our close ties to our cultures would have helped us to understand the other's perspective. Additionally, discussing future plans would have helped both of us determine if we would be able to work around our cultural differences and create our own culture to deal with our circumstances more effectively.

49

Last year Teresa and Mary attended a funeral for Mary's dad. Mary's father was Mexican and her mother is Vietnamese. Teresa brought her friend Sara to the funeral with her. Sara is Vietnamese. When it came time to console the family, Sara greeted Mary's mom with a tua. A tua is a sign of respect that young Vietnamese people show their elders. Mary's mom apparently did not see or notice Sara's greeting, and later commented to her daughter that she did not think that Sara was Vietnamese because she did not tua her. This caused tension among friends. Both Sara and Mary thought of each other as disrespectful which in turn caused problems for Teresa, who became the mediator. One result is that when Mary came over Sara's house Mary did not tua Mary's mom, which caused even more tension.

How could this problem be resolved?

Options

1. Mary could have asked Sara why she did not tua her mother, instead of working through Teresa, and that would have resolved the miscommunication.
2. The incident should have been dropped.
3. Sara should have made the tua very clear from the beginning so that Mary's mom would not have missed it.
4. Sara should apologize to Mary's mom.

Analysis of Options

1. This would have been the most direct way. Both parties may be satisfied and the issue dropped. However, such a direct approach may make both Sara and Mary uncomfortable because Vietnamese culture usually emphasizes an indirect communication style. There is a better answer.
2. This probably would not work. Both parties still would have thought of each other as disrespectful. There is a better answer.
3. If Mary's mother did not originally see the tua, Sara may not be able to make it clearer. This also does not resolve the problem since Sara cannot go back in time and do it again. There is a better answer.
4. The typical U.S. perspective would be that since Sara is not at fault she should not apologize. However, in Vietnamese culture, respect for elders is far more important than ego. Mary should recognize that although she is not wrong, apologizing would convey the appropriate respect to Mary's mom. This is the best answer.

50

My friend Mary and I have known each other since our freshman year in high school. Mary is Cambodian, and I am Filipino. Although Mary was not born in the U.S., she seemed to follow much of the American traditions. As for me, I was born and raised in the U.S. and thus followed American traditions on a daily basis.

Throughout high school, Mary and I went to all the school functions. She would go out with a guy and then the next day she would tell me all about it. The same happened when I went out with a guy. We were very dear friends.

One day in our senior year she totally surprised me when she said she was getting married. I didn't remember her telling me that she was involved or even engaged prior to this. Her explanation was that her parents had arranged her marriage. My first reaction was, "Are you going to marry him?" She said she would and she also didn't find any problems with it. Personally, I found a lot of things wrong with it.

How could you best explain this incident?

Options

1. Mary was desperate in seeking a husband.
2. I was jealous because I felt I was losing a friend.
3. I was being ethnocentric when evaluating Mary's culture concerning marriage traditions.
4. I wanted to get married before Mary did.

Analysis of Options

1. This is not an accurate response. There is no reason for this to be true.
2. This is a possible explanation because we are so close that I did not want to lose my friend, but it is not the best response.
3. This is the best response. I believe the American marriage custom in selecting your own husband is better than having a marriage partner selected for you. This is a form of ethnocentrism on my part. Although Mary has practiced many American traditions, she still believes in her culture's tradition of arranged marriages. In her eyes, her parents can make a much wiser choice in a husband than she can.
4. This is not an accurate response. I mentioned no plans to marry early.

51

My boyfriend, Edgar, and I went over to his friend, Felipe's, house. It was Felipe's birthday and everybody was meeting at Felipe's house so that we could go out and celebrate. Edgar and I were the first to arrive. We were introduced to Felipe's family, who spoke little English. Felipe's mom looked like she had just finished cooking. She asked Edgar and I if we wanted to eat. Since I had just eaten before I left the house, I politely said, "No, thank you." Unfortunately she kept on insisting that we eat. Edgar finally said, "Oh O.K., we would both like a plate." I was furious. After all I already ate, and I knew that I would not be able to finish what was put in front of me.

Why did Edgar say that he and Monica would like a plate?

Options

1. Edgar was hungry and assumed that Monica was too.
2. Edgar figured that Monica was really hungry, but she didn't want to admit it.
3. Edgar knew that they would be offending Felipe's mom if they did not eat what she had cooked.
4. Edgar thought that this would be a good way to get back at her after the fight they had had.

Analysis of Options

1. This is not the right response. There is nothing in the story to indicate that Edgar was hungry. In fact, he initially hesitated to eat.
2. This is not the correct response either. Edgar had no reason to suspect Monica was hungry.
3. This is the best response. Being that Felipe comes from a traditional Mexican family, it would have greatly offended Felipe's mom if Edgar and Monica did not eat. She had gone to the trouble of creating a nice meal, and refusing to try it is considered disrespectful.
4. There is no mention of a fight. Choose again.

52

A few months after I came to the U.S. from Japan, I made my first close American friend, Nancy, who was a very friendly, kind, and polite person. She was a serious student taking some nursing courses at San Jose State University. One day, she came over to my house to have a chat with me. We were having a nice conversation about movies, shopping, school, etc. Suddenly, she started telling me about her boyfriend. She got a picture of him out of her wallet and showed it to me, saying, "He is very cute, isn't he? Usually cute guys don't have great personalities, but he is different. He has both. He is very good-looking and also nice." Her eyes were dreamy and her face was blushed. I was surprised and looked at her strangely.

Why did I react that way?

Options

1. I was jealous of her because I didn't have a boyfriend.
2. I was surprised at the fact that Nancy made a compliment about her boyfriend.
3. I thought her boyfriend was very ugly in the picture and wondered about her taste in men.
4. I didn't believe such a perfect guy existed in the world and thought Nancy was lying.

Analysis of Options

1. Although I envied her a little, I didn't feel jealous because she was so pretty and nice that she deserved to have such a nice boyfriend.
2. This is the best answer. In Japan, people would hardly tell other people that their boyfriends or husbands are cute and it is almost as embarrassing as telling people how cute we are. I felt she was not as humble as I had thought. But later I found out that in the U.S. people usually see and respect their significant others as individuals rather than seeing those as their possessions and that it was not unusual for Americans to make a good comment about their loved ones.
3. I thought he was good-looking too.
4. I believed what Nancy said about her boyfriend was true because she had always been sincere with me.

53

My name is Rachna, and although I am Indian, I was born and raised in San Jose, California. In the summer of 1995, I decided to go visit my cousins in India. I always plan my vacation so I can celebrate my birthday in India with my cousins and family. Since I did not get a chance to celebrate my birthday with family and friends at home, my mother decided to throw me a small surprise birthday party.

On September 1st, my mother threw me a surprise nineteenth birthday party. In order for the surprise to follow through, she told me she was having my cousin and her entire family, including her mother, over for dinner. Dressed casually in jeans and a shirt, the doorbell rang at seven o'clock sharp. My mother yelled, "Rachna will you open the door please."

I thought to myself, "Why on earth does she want me to answer the door since they are her guests?" As I opened the door, there were six of my friends who yelled out surprise. My first reaction was, "Huh, why are my friends here?" Then my mother came behind me and said, "Surprise, happy birthday."

All my friends who arrived had boyfriends. Emily, my Caucasian friend, is going out with Brian, who is Chinese. Leah, who is Persian, is going out with Robert, who is Caucasian. And Carina, who is Caucasian, is going out with Tim who is half-Mexican and half-Caucasian. While sitting in the backyard, we talked amongst ourselves, waiting for dinner to be served. Quickly my mother got dinner on the table and we were seated. We ate dinner, and I asked my friends how my mother got this party organized. After dinner, I helped my mother clear the table, and rejoined my friends at the table.

During our conversation my best friend Emily started flirting with her boyfriend. While my parents were sitting in the next room she sat on her boyfriend's lap and started kissing him. My mother entered the kitchen and observed Emily's behavior and said, "Emily, there are other chairs in this house." Emily's actions made me very uncomfortable at my own party. After the party ended, my mother had a talk with me about Emily's behavior at the party.

How might you explain my reaction to my best friend's behavior?

Options
1. Rachna is jealous of her best friend's boyfriend.
2. Rachna did not have anyone to kiss on her birthday.
3. Rachna wanted to spend more time with her best friend, rather than her best friend spending time with her boyfriend at the party because it was a special day for her.
4. Since Rachna is Indian, she was embarrassed and uncomfortable by her best friend's behavior.

Analysis of Options
1. This is unlikely. All my friends had boyfriends, and there is nothing in the story to indicate I was jealous.
2. This is also unlikely. Although I didn't have a boyfriend to attend my party, I was pleased to have so many friends come and was surprised to have a party at all. There is a better answer.
3. Again, there is a better answer. Although this may be true, the story indicates I was uncomfortable by her actions. Try again.

4. This is the best answer. I felt very uncomfortable and embarrassed by my best friend's behavior because Emily's behavior was not appropriate to my family's culture. In some American households it may be acceptable to show affection towards your boyfriend in your or other's houses or in public. On the other hand, I was taught that you don't kiss, hold hands, or show any type of affection towards the opposite sex whether it is at home or in public. The way my parents raised me was that such affection is only to be displayed toward your husband in the privacy of your own home. Emily really made me uncomfortable because she disrespected my mother, my father, and myself by her actions.

54

Lisa, an American teenager, brought her friend Anna, the new transfer student from Mexico, home. Lisa's mother insisted Anna stay for dinner. As dinner was ready, Lisa's mother yelled, "Come and get it!" Lisa's family scrambled to the table, fixed their plates, and went their separate ways. Anna sat down, said grace and quietly fixed her plate. Lisa noticed Anna by herself and asked her to join her in her room to watch television while they ate. Anna looked up, shook her head and said, "No thank you." Lisa shrugged her shoulders and returned to her room.

Why did Anna stay at the table?

Options

1. She didn't like the TV show Lisa was watching.
2. She was starving and wanted to be near the food.
3. She was shocked by Lisa's family's behavior and thought they were rude.
4. She likes to eat alone.

Analysis of Options

1. This is unlikely as Anna is new to American television and probably doesn't know anything about the program.
2. This is possible, but unlikely. If Anna wanted more food she could always return to the table for seconds.
3. This is the best response. In most Mexican cultures the family always eats at the table together. Family unity and close contact is highly valued. One does not separate themselves from the family, especially at mealtime. Anna probably felt left out or ignored by Lisa and her family's independence.
4. This is unlikely, because if she felt that way Anna would not have accepted the invitation.

55

Carin, my best friend of twelve years, and I grew up together from elementary school through high school. She is of white racial background and was raised in the United States. I too was raised in the United States, yet my racial background is half Vietnamese, half white. I identify myself as Vietnamese because I follow the Vietnamese cultural roles and traditions. Because of this major cultural difference between Carin and I, we have on quite a few occasions found ourselves in awkward moments.

The first time Carin invited me over to her house to spend the night, there were several occasions where our cultural differences clashed. When I arrived at her house I met her mom and began to have a quite lengthy conversation with her. Carin kept nagging me to stop talking to her mom and to go into her room and watch a movie. I told her I wanted to continue talking to her mom because this is part of my culture, which is to respect our parents and our elders by talking, helping, and spending quality time with them. Carin was very upset that I was spending so much time with her mom and not with her, so finally I excused myself and went into Carin's room and watched our movie.

While I was in Carin's room, I heard some noise in the kitchen and assumed Carin's mom was preparing dinner, so I went into the kitchen, and sure enough dinner was being prepared. Again, out of respect, I offered to help Carin's mom prepare dinner just as I did with my mom every night. Carin's mom was surprised and delighted to have my company and help in the kitchen, so much so that she commented on the fact that she wished Carin were more helpful around the house.

A short while later Carin came downstairs to see where I had disappeared to. She came into the kitchen and was shocked that I was next to her mom chopping some vegetables. She said, "Kim, what are you doing? You don't need to help my mom. She can do that herself! Come play with me!" I didn't know what to do. I didn't want to leave Carin's mom because it's very disrespectful for the kids to not help their parents with dinner, yet on the other hand, Carin was on the verge of crying because I had barely spent any time with her.

What should I have done?

Options

1. I should have done nothing differently. I am not familiar with their culture and should have continued helping Carin's mom with dinner.
2. I should have ignored my intuition about helping her mom and focused my time with Carin.
3. I should have excused myself from chopping the vegetables and offered to help Carin with the dishes after dinner so that I could play.
4. I should have told Carin that I would play with her when I was finished helping her mom.

Analysis of Options

1. Doing nothing would have made Carin very upset and she would have probably started crying.
2. Ignoring my intuition would have been denying myself, which would have made me feel very uncomfortable the whole night.

3. This is the best answer. By excusing myself and offering to help with the dishes I am still showing respect to Carin's mom and am able to play with Carin and I would be helping Carin's chore of putting the dishes away faster.

4. Ignoring Carin's presence would have probably offended Carin's mom and also hurt Carin's feelings and I probably would have never been invited over again.

56

My friend Peggy and I have been friends for a long time. Even though I have never met her family, they know of me and I occasionally speak to them over the phone. Her mother is extremely nice to me. One night I went to Peggy's house to pick her up to go out and I finally met her mother. Her mother, who is Chinese, invited me to wait while Peggy was still getting ready. Peggy's mother offered me a drink and we began to talk. She was extremely nice to me just as she was over the phone. Then she asked me to eat with her since she had already set the table before I came. I declined but she kept persisting. Since I had already eaten before I came I could not possibly eat again. Peggy's mother said "Fine!" and abruptly took a plate of food and went to her bedroom.

Why did Peggy's mother react this way?

Options

1. She left abruptly because she suddenly remembered her favorite TV show was on.
2. Peggy's mother was offended that I did not eat with her.
3. She was just asking me to eat out of courtesy, but did not really mean it.
4. She thought that I was too skinny and that I should eat more.

Analysis of Options

1. It does not state that she went to watch TV. Please choose another option.
2. This is the best answer. In most Asian cultures, elders are very much respected. You should always try to do what is asked of you by an elder out of respect. By not agreeing to eat with Peggy's mother I was disrespecting her.
3. This could be possible, but is very unlikely. There is a better option.
4. There is no mention of weight in this story. Please choose another option.

57

Two years ago, I was commuting to the Palo Alto area and registered with the local commuter pool. I was hoping to share a ride, which would allow me to drive in the commuter lane, and shorten my 1.25-hour drive to work. A few days later, I received a call from a gentleman who indicated that his wife needed to commute to Palo Alto, just about a block from where I worked. I was invited to meet with them in their Scotts Valley home. To my delight, I was greeted at the door by a young man and woman from India. They greeted me with a smile and invited me in. I learned that Aruna did not drive, nor did her husband want her to drive Highway 17 from Scotts Valley to Palo Alto. Aruna was a doctor in India; however, it was necessary for her to complete an internship to practice medicine in the United States.

The first few days of our commute were awkward. We didn't always understand each other, even though we both spoke English. We often laughed about our misunderstandings and how we structured our sentences. The critical incident occurred when Aruna made some sweets, a delicacy from India, for me. I just took one look at them and could hardly get myself to accept them. She asked that I taste it because she had gone to great lengths to acquire some of the ingredients from a specialty store. I took a bite and it was quite awful! I said I didn't care for them, but reassured her that her toil and friendship were sincerely appreciated and that I was sure my husband would enjoy them. I thanked her for the candy. Her eyes dimmed and I saw the smile disappear from her face. That evening, I offered the candy to my husband, who seemed to enjoy them quite a bit.

The next day I presented Aruna with a box of See's candies and thanked her for her kind gesture and thoughtfulness. She smiled when I told her how much my husband liked her sweets. She quickly took a bit of the candy she selected from the See's candy box. She didn't care for the taste of the one she had picked and placed it back in the box. She looked at me, smiled, and then selected another candy, which brought a smile to her face. In the months that passed, we expressed our likes and dislikes freely.

Why was Aruna disappointed with my reaction?

Options

1. She hadn't tasted the candy before giving it as a gift.
2. She was never going to make sweets again.
3. She was angry because she spent a lot of money and time making the sweets.
4. She thought I had bad manners.

Analysis of Options

1. Aruna put so much time into purchasing the items to prepare the sweets and make them, it would be unlikely that she didn't taste them prior to giving them as a gift.
2. I doubt that she would never make sweets again, because she enjoyed cooking.
3. She probably wasn't angry, perhaps hurt.
4. She clearly stated the next day that she thought I had very bad manners. In her country, she was taught to eat everything that was offered, without commenting about one's likes or dislikes.

58

The setting is work, and after 3 months of being away, one of the workers, Ellen, is back. Ellen had talked to our boss, Kelly, about possibly having some changes made in her old schedule. Upon hearing this, another worker, Su-Kewn, realized that if Ellen got the schedule change she wanted, Su-Kewn could also get a schedule change for the better. Now, I heard the news and realized if Ellen got the hours she wanted, and in turn Su-Kewn would get the hours she wanted, then I could get the schedule change I'd been wanting. I mentioned the wonderful idea to Kelly, who realized if Ellen came in at 5 A.M., Su-Kewn could come in at 11 or 12 A.M., which would leave my time at 10 A.M. Just what everyone wanted! Kelly said she would talk to everyone later in the next week. What I realized was that I needed to know when Su-Kewn was planning to go home, or did she want to close on the days she worked. I hadn't thought about that and one or the other would determine if I got my choice of work hours or not. I found Su-Kewn the following day to ask her about it. This is how it went:

"Su-Kewn, about everyone's schedule changing, if—"
"Oh, I haven't talk to Kelly."
"I know, what I wanted to know was, what hours would *you* like to work?"
"Maybe talk to Kelly first."
"No, what I want to know is, if it were up to *you*, would—"
"I think talk to Kelly first."
"I'm not talking about making the schedule *now*, but if your schedule changes so does mine. All I want to know is, if it were up to *you*, would you stay 'till closing or leave before that?"
"If up to me, but I need to talk to Kelly before—"
"Say it was up to you. Just say it was up to you."
"Up to me, yes I will close, *but*—"
"That's *all* I was asking this *whole* time, (laugh), all I wanted to know what if it were up to *you*, if *you* had your choice would you close or not. Because—"
"Well, I think talk to Kelly first, *OK!*"

How could you best explain this incident?

Options

1. Su-Kewn really didn't understand what I meant because of language differences.
2. Su-Kewn, being an independent woman, thought I was being bossy and just used Kelly as an excuse.
3. Su-Kewn, being from a different culture, thought it was inappropriate for me, the younger one, to speak to her in such a manner.
4. Su-Kewn thought she might get into trouble if she talked to me before she talked to Kelly.

Analysis of Options

1. Although English is not Su-Kewn's native language, and she isn't fluent, she does understand it very well.
2. Su-Kewn comes from a Chinese culture where women often don't have a voice in decision making or offering opinions. But she has also seen what it is like here and has welcomed her automatic independence as a person. The biggest place she has to express this is at work and it definitely shows. I was even told by a co-worker that after I left she commented that she thought I was being bossy. This is not the right answer, but a very close second.

3. This one is correct. The rest of the day and night I felt so bad about what happened that the first thing I did when I got to work the next day was pull her aside and apologize. I told her how sorry I was for being so bossy, and she said o.k. Then she told me that she thought of me as a daughter (hugs) and just wished (tears in both of our eyes) that I would not talk so much and just listen. She was older and wiser and just wished I would listen and learn more. I told her I would keep my mouth shut more often and expressed the deep respect I held for her.

4. Su-Kewn wouldn't need to feel scared about getting in trouble. We are all a very close-knit group at work, especially with Kelly, who is the most wonderful boss in the whole world. We have talked about *everything* with each other and we are all very open with one another.

59

remember sitting in Mrs. Davis's U.S. history class my first day of high school in America after living in Hong Kong for thirteen years. My U.S. history class was my last class of the day, and it took me all day to realize why I had gotten a little bit frustrated. Throughout the day of school, I had a difficult time participating in class. I realized at the end of the day that none of my classmates raised their hands when the teacher asked a question to the class. They simply spoke without raising their hands.

Why did this frustrate me so?

Options

1. I felt that the students were simply lazy and did not feel like raising their hands.
2. I was mad because I felt that I was purposely being left out of the conversations because I was the "new kid."
3. Growing up in Hong Kong, I went to a strict school that stressed the importance of respect to the teacher, classmates, and the rules, one of which was to raise your hand before participating, otherwise you were in trouble.

Analysis of Options

1. This might be part of the reason, but it is doubtful because not all of the students were lazy.
2. Poor choice. Many of the students were very friendly.
3. This is the best answer. The teachers at my high school in California were very lax. There was more freedom in our classes in California than in Hong Kong. I was not used to freedom that the students had in the classes. I also thought that they were being rude. In Hong Kong, the teacher receives more respect, and open discussions are not encouraged. Other cultures even require that students stand when addressing their teachers, which is vastly different from the education style in the United States.

60

I was an administrative assistant in the Human Resources Department and working for a Japanese company. I consider myself to be a friendly person. Working for Human Resources, it is important that people feel comfortable with you. The building consisted of 5 floors. The 5th floor is where all of the upper management (all Japanese) worked.

Every day, as I worked in different departments, I would greet people as I passed them in the hallway with either a "hello," "good morning," "good afternoon," or "good evening." I was pulled aside one day by a co-worker who informed me that it was best not to give any type of greeting to the Japanese management, especially eye contact. It is wiser to keep your head down and not to say anything out of respect for their position.

What should I do?

Options

1. Continue to have eye contact and say "hello."
2. Say hello in Japanese—"konichi wa" with a slight bow of the head.
3. Keep my head down and say nothing.

Analysis of Options

1. This is not the best answer. To continue having eye contact and saying "hello" may only show disrespect and inconsideration. Even though a greeting is socially acceptable in our culture, to the Japanese it is considered bold.
2. This is a possible answer. I am now showing respect to the manager, and his or her culture, while keeping my own culture. I have done this not only by the gesture of bowing my head, but I have also said hello in their language. However, it is still a bold response and therefore may not be interpreted as respectful.
3. This is the best answer for I am simply following instructions and accommodating another culture. Different verbal and nonverbal behaviors symbolize respect in different cultures. If I truly want to be considered respectful and friendly, I need to adjust my behaviors to their rules.

Comments

These incidents reflect different expectations of social roles. A role is an expected set of behaviors congruent with one's position in society. A mother is expected to behave one way, children another. Students have expectations of their professors. For every position in society, there are expectations that follow. Consequently, we can see in these incidents evidence of cultural differences that influence one's expectations in dating relationships, family relationships, business relationships, and school relationships.

Incidents 40 through 48 deal with romantic relationships and the difficulties that ensue when those relationships are intercultural. Normally, romantic relationships are formed in part because people believe they have some similarities. However, intercultural differences become particularly apparent when one romantic partner begins to interact with the other's family. When a family gathers, cultural traits often become more pronounced. Additionally, one's romantic partner may be a second or third generation immigrant, making it likely that his or her parents and other family members will have more obvious cultural characteristics. Clearly then, a romantic partner may be surprised by cultural differences when finally interacting with the family.

Because of these differences, a variety of issues must be confronted. To begin, the influence of one's family differs from culture to culture. In cultures that are group oriented, the connection to one's family may be strong. Thus, one's family may play a crucial role in that individual's decisions, as demonstrated in incident 50. In cultures that are more individualistic, independence may be emphasized and decisions are made on one's own. The role of children also differs from culture to culture. Sometimes discipline, control, and respect for adults are emphasized, as we can see in incidents 43, 48, 49, 51, and 55. Other times children are encouraged to be free spirits. Additionally, attitudes toward the elderly will differ from culture to culture. Some cultures believe the elderly have a wisdom from which younger people will benefit. In these cultures the elderly are highly respected and even honored, and the elderly are expected to maintain a vital role in the family throughout their old age. Other cultures place more of an emphasis on youth. Consequently, the elderly are given less attention as they age. These different perspectives are illustrated in incidents 40 and 58.

Furthermore, gender roles may become apparent in family interactions. Often men and women will use different methods to show love and respect, and some cultures will have specific rules for men and women's behavior. For example, women may be expected to carry out specific duties such as preparing and serving men food and eating separately. Other times, individuals may take a more modern approach and expect men and women's roles to be interchangeable. As we can see in incidents 44, 45, and 46, these different expectations can be the source of confusion and even anger.

Moreover, display of affection may differ from culture to culture. Although many cultures value physical contact, the rules often change with romantic relationships. It may not be appropriate to show physical affection (i.e., hugs, kisses, sitting on one's lap, hand holding, etc.) in the presence of others. We can see the difficulties that arise from these behaviors in incidents 42 and 53.

Essentially, social roles help us to determine the appropriate respectful behavior. Consequently, as intercultural differences arise, one needs to understand *communication rules* and *accommodation*. Communication rules are, "prescriptions for behavior that indicate what is obligated, prohibited, or preferred in certain contexts" (Shimanoff, 1980). Of course, a primary difference between cultures is that they follow different rules. Therefore, to be interculturally competent, one must also be able to determine when accommodation may be appropriate. Accommodation refers to temporarily setting aside one's own communication rule to follow another's communication rule. Accommodation is usually considered respectful behavior and does help to reduce intercultural conflict and misunderstanding. However, an individual must decide when he or she is comfortable accommodating. These concepts are illustrated in incident 60.

An additional useful technique is simply to *observe and react*. Being aware of how the people around you are behaving will help you to determine what may or may not be appropriate for the situation. You can then decide to match the behavior, ask about it, or continue to follow your own rules. Because of the diversity of the United States, it is highly likely you will encounter intercultural differences in romantic relationships, school relationships, work relationships, and social relationships. Awareness will be your most useful tool.

Social Roles Exercises

Exercise 1. Personal Assessment Questions

A. Describe three rules you were taught by your parents while growing up.

_____

_____

_____

_____

_____

_____

_____

_____

B. What different social roles do you play? What behaviors accompany these roles?

roles   **behaviors**

_____

_____

_____

_____

_____

_____

_____

C. How are the elderly treated in your family?

_____

_____

_____

_____

_____

_____

_____

D. How are children treated in your family?

_____

_____

_____

_____

_____

_____

_____

E.   What activities does your whole family do together?

_____

_____

_____

_____

_____

_____

_____

F.   Do men and women behave differently in your family? If so, what are the differences?

_____

_____

_____

_____

_____

_____

G.   Pair up with a partner and describe your weekend to each other. Now, alternating roles with your partner, describe the same weekend as if you were talking to one of the following people:

parent	coworker	brother/sister
professor	neighbor	best friend
boss	town gossip	small child

How did your descriptions differ? Why?

_____

_____

_____

_____

_____

_____

_____

_____

_____

_____

_____

_____

_____

Exercise 2. Cultural Partner Question

Discuss with your partner the differences in roles and behavioral expectations between your partner's original culture and this culture. You may want to explore professional roles, family roles, social roles, etc.

Chapter Four

Culture Shock

61

After 4 months of living in California, my husband, our son, and I invited 35 people to a housewarming party in our newly rented home. We wanted to gather friends not only from Europe (Belgium, Britain, France, and Germany) but also from America and Asia. My husband contacted his colleagues at work and sent a map with directions via electronic mail while confirming the arrival time. I called mainly our personal friends and gave them directions over the phone. Thirty-five people confirmed that they would come, among them 10 Americans; so, we ordered Indian food and set up a buffet. During the party, one American couple called to let us know that they couldn't attend because of a last minute change. A second couple sent us an e-mail the following day to apologize because they couldn't make it that night. The other American persons didn't show up while all the Europeans attended.

Why did we experience such a dropout?

Options

1. The American colleagues were rude, as they didn't call to let us know.
2. Californians don't really commit even when they answer yes to an invitation.
3. The American colleagues were surprised by this invitation to our home as generally it is reserved for people they have a close relationship with and didn't really know how to respond.
4. Californians expected a more formal invitation with a clear indication that it would be a dinner party.

Analysis of Options

1. This is unlikely as they are working together daily; both these colleagues and my husband know each other and already collaborated closely in business situations. Not only would this behavior have reflected a more negative relationship but also would have jeopardized future cooperation.
2. This is not the best answer because it assumes that most Americans are not reliable or trustworthy. Furthermore, this answer only deals with one side of the situation, thus overlooking how the invitation was made. In short, this is a stereotype.
3. Even though this answer could be possible because invitation patterns are culturally bound, Californians are quite open and direct so they would have most likely declined the invitation. Again, in this specific business context, Californian colleagues and my husband work together, thus being accustomed to communicating.
4. This is the best answer. The way to invite people for a dinner party differs from one culture to another. We should have sent a written invitation with specific information about both the arrival and departure times as well as the type of party and a "RSVP" request. Not doing so most likely meant that it was an "open beer bust" where guests can stop by or not.

62

Once, an American classmate asked me if I would like to go with her to McDonald's to eat. Being from Vietnam, I was glad to have some exposure to American people and traditions. At McDonald's, we waited in line. I stood behind my friend. I was surprised when she took the tray of food, paid only for hers, and left the counter. I felt really embarrassed because I didn't bring any money to pay for the food I ordered. When the woman at the counter told me the price of the food, I had to apologize because I forgot to bring my purse. I had such a bad feeling that I dared not tell my classmate about my misunderstanding.

How can I explain this situation?

Options

1. My classmate is mean. She doesn't want to pay even though she asked me to go to eat.
2. She is not a good friend because she doesn't pay attention to me. She should wait until I get my food. I may have trouble with the way to order food or I may need her to explain the name of the food because I am new to the country.
3. I should tell my misunderstanding to her.
4. I should bring money whenever going somewhere to eat.

Analysis of Options

1. There is nothing to show whether she is mean or generous. In America, people pay money only when they treat someone. In fact, she didn't say that she invited me to McDonald's, she just asked me if I would like to go with her.
2. She probably doesn't realize that I may have difficulty. She thinks that it is easy to order food. Even if I don't understand English well, I still can show which one I want to buy.
3. I should explain my culture (person who invites pays) to her and learn about her culture. If I didn't tell her about my culture, how could she understand my behavior and how could she tell me about her culture? I should try to learn a new culture in order to accommodate to it; otherwise, I might have an incorrect opinion about human behavior and have other bad experiences. That may be the best answer.
4. Even if I think someone is going to treat me, I should always bring money with me. If I had the money, I could have paid and wouldn't have been so embarrassed. This could be a possible answer.

63

About two years ago while working at Great America in the arcades I noticed the Brazilian soccer team. While walking around I saw a young Brazilian man shoving coins into the game. I walked over to him and in very broken English he told me the game does not work. So with hand gestures I asked him to move over so I might find the problem. He gave me a funny look and then responded to my request but continued to look right over my shoulder. I checked the coin return to find many pennies, nickels, and dimes stuck in the return. I gave him back his coins and slowly tried to explain you need quarters to play, not just twenty-five cents. He then proceeded straight out of the arcade muttering angrily to himself.

How would I explain his behavior?

Options

1. The man felt offended by my use of slow speech, implying he was stupid.
2. The man felt he was ignorant for trying various coins and not a quarter.
3. The man thought that I was being rude for using hand gestures to communicate
4. The man was annoyed by having to use quarters when the slot simply asked for $.25.

Analysis of Options

1. Being from a different culture I am unaware of how to talk to a native of Brazil, which creates an obvious communication barrier. Therefore it would be very easy to offend him unknowingly. However, there is a better answer.
2. The man may have realized using a quarter was the obvious thing to do and became embarrassed at the fact. This is a possible answer.
3. Again communication rules come into place. I may have used a gesture that in his culture means something else to where he would not understand my meaning in using it. However, there is nothing in this story to indicate a specific behavior problem.
4. The man may have seen the coin slot as a very vague reference to using a quarter and felt that it was inappropriate for the slot to read $.25 instead of one quarter. This is the most likely answer.

64

Kevin went to Cabo San Lucas, Mexico for a vacation last year with his father. After two days of fun in the sun, he decided to send a few postcards back home to California. He went to a gift shop near his hotel, and browsed around before finding the perfect cards for his friends. After buying them, Kevin asked the lady behind the counter if she sold stamps. Unfortunately, she only spoke limited English, and Kevin did not know how to ask for a stamp in Spanish. He tried to use hand gestures, pointing to the area on the postcard where there is room for a stamp. The lady just shook her head and told him in Spanish that she didn't understand him. So he went on without any stamps, hoping he could get them at the hotel. In the lobby there were about fifteen people in line, waiting to speak with the receptionists behind the counter. In no mood for waiting, Kevin went to his room and wrote the cards out to his friends anyway. He put them on the table, and soon forgot about them. On the day of his departure, Kevin noticed the cards on the table, exactly where he had left them. He knew it was too late to find a post office, so he packed them up and sent them out when he got home.

How could Kevin have been better prepared to send the postcards?

Options

1. Kevin didn't need to be prepared. The lady behind the counter should have known how to speak better English, because Cabo San Lucas is a tourist town.
2. Knowing he had reservations a month ahead of time, Kevin should have brushed up on his Spanish because he was going to a foreign country.
3. Kevin could have tried a little harder to find stamps. If it was important enough, he could have found somebody who spoke both Spanish and English.
4. Kevin should not have bought the post cards in the first place.

Analysis of Options

1. Whether Cabo San Lucas is a tourist town or not, the lady behind the counter was in her native country. There is no need for her to learn the English language.
2. This would be the best answer. Kevin had plenty of time to prepare for his trip. He should have reviewed his old Spanish text book and brushed up on his vocabulary.
3. While on vacation, I would assume that most people don't want to spend their leisure time looking for stamps. He could have looked for them before he bought the cards, but how was he to know that the store would not sell stamps? There is a better solution.
4. Kevin's friends are important to him, and he wanted to show that when he bought the postcards. It makes him feel good when he sends letters or cards to friends. Although he would have rather sent the postcards while in Cabo, Kevin was content with sending them when he got home.

65

When I had just been in the United States for about one week, I went to the supermarket near my house, about seven blocks away. When I entered the door I saw people walking freely around the counters, taking whatever they wanted, and putting things into their carts. I thought in my mind, "Wow, life in the United States is so cool, people are free to choose whatever they like." So, I decided to grab a bag of chocolate. I looked around for the cashier, but I could not find him, and I saw the guard at the door. I thought I had to pay him. As I approached the door, the guard stopped me before I pulled out the money from my pocket, and told me that I had to pay at the cashier at the other door before I leave. The customers nearby were looking at me with big eyes of surprise. I felt very uncomfortable and embarrassed. I went to the cashier counter to pay for the candy I bought, and tried to leave as fast as I could. The idea of thinking life was so cool in the U.S. naturally disappeared in my head.

Why did I feel the way I did?

Options

1. The customers thought I was pretending and tried to steal things.
2. I was too cautious about these curious customers.
3. The customers would have felt it was unfair if the guard did not accuse me of trying to steal.
4. I was unfamiliar with the way business is run in America.

Analysis of Options

1. This is not a correct answer. There was no reason for the customer to think so, because I did not hide the chocolate bar as I walked toward the guard at the door.
2. While I was a bit embarrassed, my concern was more with my situation than with the customers' reactions. Choose again.
3. Please choose again. This is the guard's concern; he might or might not accuse me according to the evidence. This is not the customer's concern.
4. This is the correct answer. In my country the supermarkets are much smaller, and the customers are not allowed to walk freely around the counters to choose whatever they wanted to buy. It's completely different. This place was so big, with so many things to choose from, and I didn't even know or see where the cashier counters were. I was just overwhelmed.

66

Elizabeth, who is a French foreign exchange student living with a family in California, was generally assimilating quite well to U.S. customs. One night in the summer she and Lynn, the hosts' daughter, were helping to get dinner on the table. Lynn's mom told them to be seated as she served. The last food to reach the table was corn on the cob, to which Elizabeth let out a horrified gasp and refused to try it. Up until this point Elizabeth had tried all aspects of American culture.

Can you explain her behavior?

Options

1. Elizabeth was beginning to show signs of culture shock.
2. French are often snotty and rude.
3. Elizabeth is unfamiliar with certain foods.
4. Elizabeth feels no compulsion to please her host family anymore.

Analysis of Options

1. Not the correct response. She shows no other signs of culture shock.
2. An extremely stereotypical response and not really applicable; choose again.
3. This is the correct response. In France corn is only to feed pigs. Elizabeth, at Lynn's request, finally tried it cut off the cob. She liked it so much she requested it often and took seeds home with her to France and planted them.
4. The French are usually very gracious to their hosts.

67

I couldn't wait for this day to come. It was the day my foreign exchange student was to arrive from Finland. I had all these things planned to show her, and I couldn't wait for her to meet my friends. I was not worried if we would get along or anything. I was just excited she was coming. I wasn't even worried that we wouldn't be able to communicate because everyone in his or her program was supposed to speak English.

We went to where we were supposed to pick her up, and we had to stand in line until we could get to the table to tell them our name. Then we would meet Heidi. All the exchange students were sitting in this room looking at all the people as one by one their name was called and they would stand up and meet their host family. As I stood in line with my mom and my brother, I was scanning the room trying to figure out which one was Heidi. Finally, it was our turn and the guy at the table shouted, "These are the Fergusons, for Heidi." This really tall girl who had bright red hair stood up and walked over to us. She seemed really different from the picture they sent to us, but I knew people changed. I was a little shocked by the way she looked, but I was still very excited about her arrival. As we walked to the car we tried to talk to her, and it was then we realized she didn't speak English as well as we thought she could. She seemed to be shy and scared, but that didn't bother me because I knew if I was in her position I definitely would have been scared.

I had a really large room that Heidi and I were going to share. I had totally rearranged it and set up my trundle bed for her. I also had made space for her in my closet. I was really proud of the way my room looked and everything I had done, but she didn't seem at all impressed. I think about this time I was getting extremely nervous and this was the first time I started thinking, "What if we don't get along? What if we have nothing in common?" I was trying to make small talk to her and she kept answering me with short one-sentence answers or nothing at all. I just thought she must be tired and thought things would get better.

That's when the first thing that happened that totally appalled me. We were having dinner and right at the dinner table she pulled out a needle and some insulin and lifted up her shirt and gave herself a shot. I knew she was diabetic and had no problem with that because my aunt is also diabetic and as a child she would let me give her shots sometimes. But, that was only in the privacy of her bedroom, never at the dinner table. Things from there just got worse. She had only one friend in the program with her and she always came over to our house. That was fine too except we would all be in my room and they would talk in Finnish, and not include me at all. It made me feel like an outsider in my own room.

I still wasn't giving up yet. I always invited her over to do things with me and my friends and she would come along and never say anything. She wouldn't even walk with us; she would walk a few steps behind us. It was then I decided that I didn't like her very much because I thought I was trying hard to include her and she wasn't trying at all. I guess at that point I also realized that we had nothing in common, and probably gave up on trying to be her friend. We didn't like the same kind of music, like the same kind of clothes, weren't interested in the same things and I was trying and she was not. When her friend was over and they were talking away in Finnish I could occasionally even hear my name, so to me that meant they were talking about me. And I couldn't understand this because I was always trying and she wasn't trying to get to know me. I felt like it was a stab in my back.

How could I have prevented this awful situation?

Options

1. I could have had smaller expectations for her when she arrived. If I would have had smaller expectations then I wouldn't have been as disappointed when things didn't go the way I expected.
2. Before she came I could have studied up on the Finnish culture. I could have taken a class on intercultural communication before she came.
3. I could have told her that some of the things she was doing were not considered appropriate in my culture, and that they were considered rude. Also, I should not have jumped to any conclusions about how the rest of her stay was going to be like. I could have tried to help her learn what is considered appropriate here instead of assuming she would already know.
4. I could have not even tried from the start. The first time she did something wrong, I could have judged her from then on and just ignored her.

Analysis of Options

1. Even though some would consider this to be true, there is a better answer. Choose again.
2. This also would have been a good choice, but I didn't have the option of taking this class, or even the knowledge that our cultures would be that different. So, there is a better answer. Choose again.
3. This is the best answer. Instead of expecting her to know what was considered right I could have told her even though I was afraid this would have been considered rude. After the first two weeks I should have not given up because that just set up a bad mood for the next three weeks of her visit. After all, she was my visitor, and I had the responsibility of being her mentor in a new culture. I should have kept trying and things might have changed instead of getting worse.
4. This obviously is not an appropriate choice because everyone deserves a second chance.

68

I met another student at the beginning of the quarter, a girl named Mabel from Taiwan. She had problems getting a good hold on the English language, and as the quarter progressed we studied together, and a friendship kind of developed. I have a culturally mixed group of friends that I have known for some time now. We have a Friday night ritual, in which we all get together and have dinner and catch up about what is new in our lives for the week. Small things like work, school, promotions and birthdays are discussed, and most of the time we find some other activity also, like going to see a movie, playing pool, out to night clubs, etc. Occasionally, the members of this group will invite new people to join us, and if the group generally accepts that person, they also may become a "regular" to these gatherings. Most of the group members are Asian-American, we're all in our 20's, and most of us have degrees and are working in professional jobs. I'm the only member that is still attending college.

I invited Mabel to join our group on a few occasions, and she accepted. The nature of the group is very dynamic; not everybody will make it every week. Some people travel or have other engagements, and the only time the group really gets together as a whole is for an important event like somebody's birthday. Anyhow, Mabel seemed to enjoy the group, and the group enjoyed having her.

Well, the misunderstanding took place Friday night as we were getting together. I went to pick up Mabel. As we were leaving her place, she asked for the names of the people that would be at the outing that evening. When I told her the names, she changed her mind about coming out with us, and asked me to take her home. I didn't think much of it, so I complied. When I got to the group, they asked where Mabel was, as I told them I was bringing her. So I described to them what had occurred, then they asked me about the motive. "Was she sick? Did she not feel well?" I replied "no" as she did not seem ill, she just asked who was going to be there then when I answered she asked that I take her home. Well, this offended the members of my group a great deal.

One member stated, "What, does she think she is too good for us?" Another member, who is Chinese-American, shared his stereotype about Taiwanese people. He said that Taiwanese people are snobs. They are really Chinese, everything about them is the same as Chinese culture, but they think they are better than regular Chinese because they are wealthy. There are two main dialects in Chinese culture, Cantonese and Mandarin. The majority of Chinese people speak one dialect very well and the other not so well, depending on where in the country you live. He said that a Taiwanese person he knew said that Mandarin was "the only PROPER Chinese language, and that Cantonese was the language of barbarians." This is because they only speak Mandarin in Taiwan.

So since Mabel was Taiwanese, the group members interpreted her action as typical of people from her country. Needless to say, they were not happy about this, and they asked me not to invite her back to the group. This bothered me because up to this point in time Mabel had not displayed any of the stereotypical behaviors described above, and I like to think the best of people, but as the night wore on the things that my friends said began to bother me more and more. I have known these friends for many years, we have all been through the good times and bad times together, and I really place a high level of value and trust on their opinions.

So as the night ended, I decided to have a "come to Jesus meeting" with Mabel. In the high-tech business world a "come to Jesus meeting" is where all the people involved in a problem or project get together to clear the air. There are no ranks in these meetings, you can be free from the fear of saying something bad about an important person, and having that person fire you. The task is to come clean, reveal all secrets, and discuss all issues that may be bothering people. They are generally very constructive.

So the next day I asked Mabel for clarification on her actions, during which time I was brutally honest about what had occurred and how the group reacted. In American culture, brutal honesty is valued. It is not an easy thing to do, to bring uncomfortable subject matter to the surface for discussion. Needless to say, Mabel reacted with anger, saying things like, "you are very cruel to talk about this." Now, I tried my best to tell her that this was the group's impression of what had occurred, and that I at first did not share that opinion, but as I looked for the motive behind her actions, the group's impression gradually became my own. In Taiwanese culture you never discuss such things as it is considered rude and you would lose face.

She finally replied that some of the people in our group are dating, and she felt uncomfortable around them because they hold hands, hug, and kiss each other in public. Apparently, in Taiwan, couples do not display affection in public. Well, as a result of this exchange, she became really upset, and said that my actions had reinforced her stereotype that all American people were bad people. She asked to end the friendship and she made a comment to the effect that she will never have another American friend again.

My take on friendship is that sometimes you will do things with your friends that you may not really want to do, but you do anyway to be a friend. For instance, some of the group members like to see certain types of movies, whereas other members may not want to see them, but we go along anyhow in the name of friendship. Mabel's perspective was that she was unwilling to do anything that made her uncomfortable.

Looking at it now from another angle it seems Mabel chose separation. She decided some time ago that even though she is in America, she will keep her Taiwanese culture. To me that option seems very closed-minded. If you want to keep your original culture, why bother going to another country? My mindset is that if I went to another country, I would try my best to perform some uncertainty reduction about the native culture, and eventually I would try to integrate into it.

So this exchange ended rather poorly. Mabel said that she regretted all the time we spent together, and that she wished that she never met me. I, on the other hand, do not regret the time spent with her, but I was a bit upset with myself that I was not able to identify earlier that she choose separation as a means to deal with her culture shock. My mistake was that I suffered from the projective cognitive similarity, where I thought I could show her a bit of the Asian-American culture that I belong to in order to broaden her horizons.

Coming out of this situation, the group I belong to seems even more entrenched in their prejudice about Taiwanese people. The events that transpired only reinforced their viewpoint. On the other side of the spectrum it would seem that I confirmed Mabel's prejudice about American people. For me, I must admit I have entertained the thought that what my friends said about Taiwanese people is true, but I would still like to think that people are individuals, and that it cannot be that every Taiwanese person is this way. It just happens that the Taiwanese people that my friends and I encountered thus far are this way. I think in the future I will be a bit more wary of Taiwanese people, but I still refuse to believe that all Taiwanese people are like Mabel.

Comments

These incidents reflect the difficulties people have adjusting to new cultures. Being in a new culture requires one to adjust to new rules and unmet expectations. This can be confusing and incredibly frustrating. People transition through cultures throughout their lives. While many of our subjects in these incidents have moved to a new country, moving to a new college or starting a new job can also present some very similar obstacles. Culture shock is the frustration and confusion that result from receiving uninterpretable cues. Consequently, any new environment that demonstrates different cultural characteristics is likely to produce culture shock. The typical model to describe culture shock is the U Curve (Oberg, 1960), as seen below.

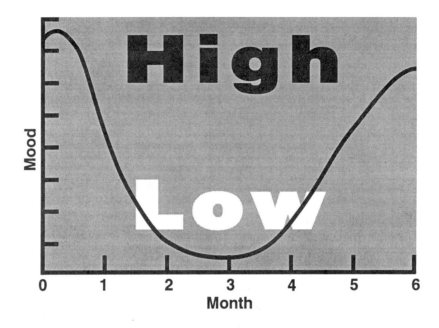

According to the U Curve theory, people go through an adjustment period once immersed in a new culture. In the first few months, one's mood drops dramatically. Initially, people are usually excited to be in a new culture for a variety of reasons. However, people realize quickly that adjusting is more difficult than they imagined and they essentially become homesick. Thus, at approximately 3 months into the new culture, emotions become increasingly negative. Additionally, our bodies respond to those negative emotions, making the whole process even more difficult to bear. The intense emotions we experience during this low point are called *affective experiences* (Moghaddam, Ditto, and Taylor, 1990). These can include depression, paranoia, anger, and frustration, among others. Corresponding to our affective experiences are *somatic changes* (Cushner and Brislin, 1996). A somatic change is how our body responds to our negative emotions. This can include headaches, insomnia, increased blood pressure, digestive difficulties, lack of appetite, etc. Because of these intense emotions and physical problems that are often difficult to diagnose, people sometimes give up on their new culture and "go home." Incidents 63, 65, 66, and 68 illustrate the ineffective reactions people have in certain situations because of their culture shock. Clearly, people experiencing culture shock are more likely to engage in *fundamental attribution error*.

Fortunately, as you can see in the graph above, people do eventually adjust to their new culture. Eventually those uninterpretable cues become interpretable. People begin to understand the ways of doing things, the language or jargon, the predominant values, the style of living, etc. People also begin to form friendships and feel like they have a group that they belong to again. Consequently, the mood begins to elevate and eventually adjusts to a normal level.

However, waiting for time to pass is not the most proactive method to reduce culture shock. Especially when one is aware of their culture shock, there are other techniques he or she can utilize to help the adjustment process.

Martin and Nakayama refer to the *fight or flight* response when adapting to a new culture. In the fight approach, people involve themselves as much as they can in their new culture, making new friends, trying new foods, learning the language, etc. Consequently, the fight approach requires that people communicate more with members of the new culture. People who use this approach will engage in *uncertainty reduction* (Berger and Calabrese, 1975). Uncertainty reduction results from the desire to predict and understand how people will behave in particular situations. Therefore, to gain this information, people might ask questions as they interact with people from the new culture or seek out a mentor to explain the cultural rules. The fight approach risks making some intercultural mistakes, and will probably increase culture shock in the short term.

In the flight approach, people limit their involvement in a new culture and simply observe and learn until they are comfortable interacting. In this case, uncertainty reduction strategies take a more passive role. We can see this process in incidents 64 and 67. While this may postpone culture shock, it also limits the opportunities to learn about a new culture. Most people will probably choose a combination of these methods depending upon their own individual preferences and the conditions within the surrounding environment.

Furthermore, as people begin to socialize within their new culture on a long term basis, there are some specific choices to be made about how one wants to position him or herself within the larger society. If people want to hold on to their original culture and isolate themselves from the new culture, they may choose *separation*. Separatists will choose to interact only with people from their original culture, will continue to communicate in the style of their original culture, and will avoid interaction with people from the new culture as much as possible. For some people this is a more pleasant alternative than culture shock, but it obviously can make practical living difficult. The opposite approach is *assimilation*. Assimilation is immersing oneself completely into the new culture to the point of losing or ignoring one's original culture. Whereas this makes interaction in the new culture easier, many people are uncomfortable giving up their original culture entirely. An alternative to these two approaches is *integration*. With the integration approach, people maintain their original culture and also interact with people from the new culture. In short, integrators choose the best of both worlds. However, this approach may be more difficult or confusing because it requires more flexibility. Finally, people may believe that they don't belong anywhere. This position is called *marginalization*. Marginalized people believe they have lost ties to their original culture, but don't quite fit into the new culture either. Marginalization is usually difficult and frustrating for those who experience it. Consequently, marginalized people usually make efforts to find a culture in which they feel they belong.

Clearly, these different stages of adjustment are going to influence interaction. If one is experiencing culture shock, they may respond more emotionally and more negatively to situations, as we can see in incidents 62, 65, and 68. The receivers of these responses, because they do not understand their communication partner's situation, often make assumptions in the form of fundamental attribution error or stereotypes that further complicate communication. This is illustrated clearly in incident 67. Additionally, individual socialization choices will influence whether or not interaction takes place at all. As we can see in incident 68, it appears that Mabel has chosen to isolate herself and avoid future interaction with Americans.

Understanding these complications that come with adjustment to a new culture assists not only those who have to adjust but also those who interact with them.

Culture Shock Exercises

Exercise 1. Experiencing Culture Shock

A.   Attend a cultural event. Your task is to attend an event that revolves around a culture with which you are not familiar. In fact, it should be a culture that is very different from your own. However, you probably do not have to stray too far outside of your community to find it. For example, you may choose to attend a social event that you would not normally go to (i.e., a bowling event, a rave, a country bar, a marathon, etc.), to attend a festival intended for members of that culture (i.e., a Pow Wow, Chinese New Year celebration, etc.), to attend a religious ceremony you are not familiar with, to attend a community event in another town . . . . You have a lot of *options*; be creative.

As you are selecting an event, take note of your feelings and responses. Do you feel silly even choosing one? Are you nervous or afraid? Is it exciting? Are you procrastinating? Make notes below.

As I plan my cultural event, I feel . . .

B. During the event. Once you are actually there experiencing the event you have chosen, be aware of your reactions again. Take notes that will help you answer the following questions.

What aspects of others' behavior stand out the most?

_____

_____

_____

_____

_____

How are you behaving?

_____

_____

_____

_____

_____

How are you feeling?

_____

_____

_____

_____

_____

Are you showing how you are feeling?

_____

_____

_____

_____

What coping strategies are you using to help you adjust?

_____

_____

_____

_____

_____

_____

_____

C. **After the event.** You made it! Now that you have experienced your event, answer the following questions:

Are you glad you did it?

_____

_____

_____

_____

_____

Would you do it again?

_____

_____

_____

_____

_____

Do you feel differently now than you did before or during the event? How so and why?

_____

_____

_____

_____

_____

_____

_____

_____

_____

_____

_____

What has this taught you about future interactions with foreign cultures?

_____

_____

_____

_____

_____

_____

_____

Exercise 2. Sharing Your Culture

Share with the class an activity that you engage in through one of your cultures. It should be an activity that everyone can participate in, and should not take longer than 20 minutes. Afterwards, discuss how you felt sharing it and how the class felt about participating.

Exercise 3. Personal Assessment Questions

A.   What experiences have you had with culture shock? How did you react?

_____
_____
_____
_____
_____
_____
_____
_____
_____
_____
_____
_____
_____
_____

B.   Help someone else who is going through culture shock. It may be a new classmate, someone new in your neighborhood, etc. How did you help that person adapt? How did you feel?

_____
_____
_____
_____
_____
_____
_____
_____
_____
_____
_____
_____
_____
_____
_____
_____
_____

Exercise 4. Cultural Partner Question

It is very likely your cultural partner experienced culture shock. Discuss this with him or her. You may want to ask the following questions:

- When did you experience culture shock?
- What was most difficult about it?
- How did you feel?
- How did you react?
- What did you do to cope?
- Do you still feel it now?

Chapter Five

Judgments

69

For the past two years I have enjoyed playing on an adult, co-ed softball team. Everyone is very supportive and is playing to have fun. The team is well mixed with many different races. The first night I got to meet my teammates I was a little uncomfortable because I was the new kid. Before the game started I got the chance to meet a young woman. She was about twenty-six years old. She had light brown skin and short wavy hair. I figured she was Hawaiian or maybe Mexican. At the end of the game the team was crowded around the bleachers socializing. Some were talking about highlights of the game and others were just taking off their cleats, putting on their tennis shoes. The young woman motioned me over to her and introduced me to her parents who had come to watch her. I was surprised to find out that she actually wasn't Hawaiian or Mexican, but actually half-black and half-white. I was so shocked that I said to her, "You don't look black at all." The young woman gave me a funny look and said, "Yep, I've heard that before." She shook her head and turned away. I didn't understand what had just happened. I felt bad for blurting out an obviously upsetting comment.

Why did the young woman react as though she was uncomfortable or upset?

Options

1. She was just tired and wanted to go home.
2. She felt what I had said was hurtful and racist.
3. She was mad and never wanted to speak to me again.
4. She understood it was a common reaction and that I didn't know it was a sensitive area I had fallen into.

Analysis of Options

1. The fact that she is tired and wanted to go home may be true, but it is not the reason she reacted to the comment in a negative way. If she were that tired, she probably would not have made the effort to introduce me to her parents.
2. This answer is a little harsh. The young woman may have been hurt by what I had said, but cannot tell if I am a racist by an innocent observation like the one I made.
3. This answer is also a little extreme. This is not the first time that she has heard this comment about her appearance. She may have learned to try to ignore it. She doesn't turn away from the situation because she hates the person and doesn't want to speak to them again.
4. This is the best answer. She reacted the way she did because she understood that I didn't know it was a sensitive issue. She shook her head and turned away as a nice way of showing me what I had said hit a sensitive spot. She didn't want to discuss it right away, so she could think of a way to explain why she reacted the way she did.

70

Marilyn, Tony, and I had just met at our new job orientation. The next evening the three of us were driving on our way to Richmond for two days of intensive job training. The long drive gave us an opportunity to get to know each other. As we listened to a variety of music on Marilyn's tape, she told us how much she enjoyed reggae music because it reminded her of her native Jamaica. Tony added that he favored contemporary soul music because he loved to dance, and that it was the next best thing to real soul food. Then he asked me what kind of music I liked. I said I was developing an interest in contemporary jazz and added that my son was beginning to take saxophone lessons. I went on to describe my son's outstanding music teacher who was a dynamic, talented, 6-foot-10-inch-tall "Afro American," who magically captured the attention of all his young students. At that moment, Marilyn's eyes left the road. She turned toward me with a look of shock and disbelief. I sat humble and frozen and didn't say another word.

Why was Marilyn so disturbed?

Options

1. Marilyn was shocked at my fondness for jazz and felt badly that she didn't bring enough saxophone music.
2. Marilyn was on a manhunt and the music teacher sounded like the man of her dreams.
3. Marilyn was disturbed because this 6-foot-10-inch tall "Afro American" was wasting his time teaching music to grade school children when he could be making his fortune playing professional basketball.
4. Marilyn was offended by my effort to be politically correct by using the term "Afro-American" to describe the music teacher.

Analysis of Options

1. This is not the right response. There was not indication that the tape did not exclude saxophone music.
2. This is not correct. Marilyn's love life was not a part of the conversation.
3. This is not correct. There is nothing in the story about basketball.
4. This is the best response. Marilyn was disturbed because I referred to the teacher as being "Afro-American." Marilyn felt comfortable enough to tell me that the term was incorrect. She explained that the word, "afro" is a hairstyle, not a race. She further added that abbreviating African to Afro was an insult to the people of African descent. She explained that the term "Afro American" would be the same as saying "Mex American" or "Jap American". The term "African American" is appropriate for those whose origin is Africa.

71

Often I accompany my mother to the grocery store. My mother was born here in the United States, but is of Mexican descent. My mother speaks perfect English with no accent; she also speaks Spanish with no accent and French with a mixed American/Spanish/French accent. However, on many occasions, the checkstand clerks decide that they want to speak to me instead of to my mother. They ask me if I want paper or plastic; they tell me how much the total is, so I can tell my mother, who understands perfectly. My mother has always allowed me to respond for us. I say thank you and we leave.

The checkout clerks talk to me because:

Options
1. They like to talk to children because it makes them happy to talk to kids.
2. They talk to the first person in line.
3. They think that all Mexican people cannot speak English, but their children can.

Analysis of Options
1. This is possible, because many people do like to talk to children. However, in this case, it would be more proper to speak to the adult.
2. This is possible too. They could have thought that I was buying all the family groceries. However, this is also incorrect, since I was too young to be in a store by myself, let alone buy the family groceries.
3. This is the most appropriate assumption. Many people make the decision that if you look foreign, then you do not speak English.

72

About two years ago, when I was working at a Costco store in the security department, I experienced a situation of miscommunication between a customer and myself. My duties during that time were to check the receipts of members leaving the store with groceries to ensure that their purchases were neither over or under charged. It happened quite often. As well, I was instructed to check all large bags (backpacks, diaper, and stroller bags) to prevent theft. This part of the job really made me feel extremely uncomfortable. It made the members perceive that we (the workers) did not trust them. I would check everyone's bag as quickly and discretely as possible, smiling and being friendly, to make them understand that this was just a standard operating procedure for the store.

One day when the lines were really backed up I was there at the door checking receipts by myself. I was in a hurry to get everyone out as quickly as possible and check the bags at the same time. This one Hispanic couple who walked past me did not understand that I needed to check her diaper bag. She must not have understood English as I asked as politely and smilingly as possible to see if I could check it. Because the lines were long and I was getting backed up, I did not wait for her permission and just quickly checked it. Of course, there was nothing in the bag, but the wife informed the husband and he became extremely upset about he incident. He did not see and hear me asking permission to check and when he was aware of what I did, he assumed that I was doing so because they were Hispanic.

He quickly walked over to the membership department and began filing a complaint about me. My lines were still backed up at the time, but I took time out to explain to him that it was my job to check all bags. He refused to listen and insisted that I only checked his bag because he was Hispanic. I informed my supervisor, who was also Hispanic, of the incident and he was able to talk to the member and make him understand that I was only doing my job and I checked all bags regardless of a member's race.

How could I have avoided this incident?

Options
1. I should have waited until the wife consented to let me check the bag before I did anything no matter how hurried I was.
2. I should have spoken more slowly or gotten a translator.
3. I should have confirmed their understanding that this was a routine procedure.
4. I should have done nothing differently. It just goes with the territory.

Analysis of Options
1. This is not a good option. Even with her consent, there still may be the misunderstanding of motive.
2. Speaking more slowly might help with people who do not speak English fluently, but then I would have to guess who speaks English and who doesn't, and I could easily offend someone. Providing a translator for every language I might encounter would be costly and unrealistic. There is a better answer.
3. This is the best option. Despite my hurry, taking the time to make sure they understood that I do this with everyone, before searching the bag, would have helped significantly. I could have asked questions or looked for nonverbal cues to ensure they understood.
4. This is not a good option. While there will always be communication problems when dealing with a diversity of cultures, we need to try to solve them, not ignore them. Choose again.

73

The following incident has happened to me at least 10 times, if not more, in all different types of settings. The first time this happened to me was about 6 years ago. I was walking into the bank to deposit some money. The bank teller was obviously Filipino, because she had the same dark features as myself.

The minute I walked up to the counter, she smiled and said, "Are you Filipinas?"

I smiled back and said, "Yes, I am."

The bank teller immediately started speaking Tagalog (one type of dialect from the Philippines) really fast and I think asked me a question because she waited for me to say something.

I looked at her puzzled and said, "What did you say? I'm from America."

All of a sudden, she frowned and asked me, "You do not speak Tagalog?"

And I said, "No, I was raised here."

Immediately her face contorted into what I consider a "snotty" look and she said, "Oh, you're one of *those*—Americanized."

I wasn't sure whether to take this offensively or not, but for some reason I did. I immediately shot back to her "I'm proud to have been born and raised in America."

She had no response to that and just continued with my transaction. There was definitely tension in the air and from that point on, neither of us tried to converse with the other.

What was the cause for this miscommunication?

Options
1. The bank teller was not very fluent in English and could not understand my response.
2. I was ashamed of being Filipino and did not want to admit it.
3. I thought the bank teller was being rude for assuming that I spoke Tagalog.
4. The bank teller thought that I was being condescending for telling her that I was from America—implying that she wasn't "from here," thus immediately starting the breakdown of communication.

Analysis of Options
1. There was no indication that she was not fluent in English because she was able to ask questions correctly. Also, working in a bank in America you would have to be fluent in English.
2. Although I may not have strong cultural ties to the Philippines, I definitely was not ashamed of my heritage. I had proudly answered "Yes" when she asked me if I was Filipinas.
3. This could be the answer but is not the best possible solution. There was more to the situation that just her being angry that I did not speak Tagalog.

4. The is the best possible answer. Our conversation had started out with good intentions of making polite conversation and maybe finding something in common, but, when she started speaking Tagalog, I became irritated that she would assume something about me without knowing me. To me, that was stereotyping. She immediately saw the frown on my face, and interpreted that to mean that I did not want to associate with speaking the language. And finally, when I responded to her "I'm from America," it made her feel as if I was excluding her from this country. In fact she could have been born and raised here as well, but was bilingual. It is very easy for us to assume what culture each of us are from just by physical appearances, but the best way to be interculturally competent in this situation is to ask and find out. People would probably welcome your questions much quicker than if you were to prejudge them.

74

In almost every job I have had, I have always been asked if I speak Spanish. I guess it's natural for people to ask this question because I am Mexican American. Unfortunately, my parents failed to teach me the language so I've lost that part of my culture. It is a given that people would become a little upset that I wouldn't be able to communicate with them, especially if they are trying their best to speak English to me.

About a year ago I had a part-time job working as a bank teller. The areas of my branch had a lot of people who spoke only Spanish, so when they would come up to me they would automatically speak Spanish to me. I remember a couple who approached my window and asked me if I spoke Spanish and I replied no. All of a sudden they started talking about me in Spanish saying that I was white washed and that I lost the knowledge of where I came from. I replied to the conversation and told them, "I understand Spanish, but I can't speak it." The couple looked very surprised and spoke to me in English for the rest of their transaction. At this point, I felt hurt and upset because these two complete strangers just didn't know me at all to make a comment like that.

Why did the couple behave the way they did?

Options
1. The couple probably only spoke Spanish instead of English and it upset them when I couldn't speak Spanish.
2. The couple thought I was too Americanized and embarrassed of my ethnicity.
3. The couple was having a bad day and may have encountered the same situation somewhere else.
4. The couple didn't think to ask if I was from the United States and if that was the reason why I didn't learn Spanish.

Analysis of Options
1. This could not have been the case because as soon as the couple found out I understood them they began to speak good English.
2. This couldn't be correct because they never asked me what nationality I was, and for all they knew I could have been Italian, and I never gave the impression I was better than they were.
3. Although this sounds like a good answer, it's not the solution because if they attempted to speak Spanish in another store and failed, it should have given them a clue that the majority of people are going to speak English in a store or a bank, so instead of getting themselves all upset they should just stick to English.
4. This would be the simplest and nicest way to respond to my incident because I could have explained to the couple that I was born and raised in the United States and grew up in an area with a large majority of English-speaking families. Because of this, my parents only spoke English in my home, so naturally that is my first and unfortunately my only language.

75

Dan was born in the Philippines but was raised in San Francisco. A music lover who particularly listened to punk and ska and expressed himself through the music he listened to, he wore chains that would hang on the side of his pants, bracelets, baggy pants, band t-shirts, and last but not least, colored his hair different colors now and then (green to purple, red to yellow, etc.). Dan knew that he was different from other Filipinos. He hung around particularly with white guys who shared the same interests in music and skateboarding.

At the school Dan attended, there were many cliques, or groups of different cultures, races, religions, etc. These groups all hung around in different areas in the school. Dan was a socializer who loved to say "What's up?" to everyone he knew. But Dan was always hesitant to go to the Filipino crowd and say "Hi" to his old friends. One day Dan walked through the Filipino clique with his girlfriend Laney, who was blond and a skater betty. When Dan stopped over to say hi to his old friend Ricky, he felt such bad vibes. He felt eyes staring at him and voices saying "weirdo." He heard people talking in Tagalog and he somewhat understood what they were saying. Dan heard such sayings as "This Filipino is a whitewash," or "This guy forgot his culture." They ridiculed his clothes, his white girlfriend, and most of all Dan's individuality. When Dan and Laney walked away, he felt awful that his own race would deny him and talk trash behind his back.

What reasons would you give Dan for his apparent ostracism by his own race?

Options

1. They were jealous of his individuality and his pretty blond girlfriend.
2. They probably thought Dan's behavior and style was just a show-off.
3. They were intolerant of a Filipino who seemed to be a bit different from the fairly rigid norms of behavior and appearance.
4. They were offended because Dan stopped hanging around Filipinos and hung out with the skateboarders.

Analysis of Options

1. This may not be true of all the Filipinos in the group to react in the same manner as some of the rude ones did. There is a better explanation. Please choose again.
2. It may be a possibility that they were acting up on Dan because they thought he was a big show-off with his style, but if that was true then the group wouldn't have stared so hard and given Dan more attention. There is a more complete explanation.
3. This is the best explanation. Many cultures are quite intolerant of people who appear to deviate too far from the behavioral norms of the majority. As a result, that particular person will often suffer from ridicule and exclusion from the group, especially if you deviate from your own race and set your own culture that involves other races. In Dan's situation, he hung around with his peers that held the same interests as his, and the majority of skaters that listen to ska music are white. Dan should understand the Filipinos' responses because he was out of the norm.
4. They would feel somewhat offended that a Filipino is hanging around the white crowd, but they should know the fact that culture is learned and that Dan's interests in skateboarding and music fit him into a category in which the majority of the group is white. However, he did not choose that crowd because they were white. This is a good explanation, but there is a better one.

76

While growing up in Hawaii the local people there, including myself, enjoyed the dish sushi. It is a delicacy that has been adapted from Japan and adopted as one of our own popular dishes on the island. There has been a misconception that sushi's main ingredient is raw fish, explaining why many people do not try the dish.

After high school, I re-located to California, where I live with my sister, Sharlotte. I was fortunate to get a job at the same place where Sharlotte was working, but in a different department. Since we worked together, we would often take breaks and lunch together. Sometimes I would get to the lunchroom before Sharlotte and would start eating without her. However, on one particular day, four other employees from Sharlotte's department occupied the table next to mine.

While I was eating my lunch, I overheard one of the ladies say to another, "Look, she's eating sushi." She then turned her head and looked at me as if I was an alien. The co-worker responded, "Isn't that raw fish?" And one of the ladies said, "Yes, it is and you would never catch me eating that." Their conversation was loud enough that I could hear each of them. Being a new employee of the company and from a different department, I pretended that I did not hear the comments that they were expressing. I could sense that they were looking at me which made me feel very uncomfortable. As a result, I began to lose my appetite.

Just when I was about to gather my lunch together, Sharlotte finally showed up and joined me, which made me feel at ease. Since the ladies knew Sharlotte, they asked her what she was having for lunch. Sharlotte's response was, "teriyaki beef sushi." The same lady who made the comment about my lunch, made a facial expression of dislike. Upon seeing that, Sharlotte told her, "Do you know what sushi is? You're probably thinking it's a dish of raw fish and somebody probably told you that."

The co-worker nodded and pointed at the other co-worker, accusing her of that. Sharlotte then went over to her table and showed them what a sushi is and explained to them the ingredients that make up sushi. She also assured them that not all sushis are raw fish and there is a wide variety to choose from. Astounded and in awe by Sharlotte's explanation, they were all quiet. After, Sharlotte offered each a sushi, but they all declined and stated that they were full from their lunch and maybe would try it next time.

Sharlotte responded with a famous line that my father used to tell us while growing up, "You don't know what you're missing until you try it." They all smiled, and went back to work while Sharlotte joined me at the table and began feasting on her teriyaki beef sushi. She also explained the reactions from her co-workers.

What explanations did Sharlotte give about her co-workers' attitudes?

Options
1. The co-workers had difficulty accepting what sushi is and that they were embarrassed to give it a try.
2. The ladies only accepted what they heard from others, that sushi only contains "raw fish." As a result, their misconception of sushi restricted them from trying it.
3. The co-workers wanted attention, so they reacted the way they did to a new employee.
4. The co-workers wanted to have fun and gossip during their lunch hour, so they talked about the new employee eating the sushi even though they all knew all about sushi.

Analysis of Options

1. There were no signs of embarrassment, but signs of surprise of knowing that sushi are not only made with raw fish. Please choose again.
2. This is the best answer. Although the co-workers had seen an actual sushi indicating no raw fish, they had come to the conclusion that it contained a specific ingredient that most people would never attempt to eat, raw fish. Their attitudes and beliefs of others probably influenced the group's behavior that none of them wanted to try it.
3. There were no indications that any of them wanted attention from others in the lunch room. Please try again.
4. The co-workers did not know that other ingredients could make up sushi. When Sharlotte showed them the sushi, their facial expressions showed how surprised they were to find that out. By this, we can not assume that they did know all about the dish, sushi. Please choose again.

77

It was a relaxing sunny day lounging by the pool. In the summer many people from the apartment complex would come to socialize and have a good time. Today the party consisted of my cousin Tommy, three older neighbors, Pete, Mike, and Paul, the off-duty apartment handyman, and John, who was Mexican American. Hours went by as we discussed funny stories and sports, when suddenly a bearded man approached us, provoking a warm round of greetings from Pete, Mike, and Paul. Although I did not recognize him, the greetings and the man's smile indicated he was friendly.

As he began to speak, I realized the man was Russian and spoke no English. John interrupted him harshly as he introduced himself to my cousin and I, saying, "No! No! Get out of here! I told you you can't be out here! Go back to Russia!"

The Russian man looked puzzled and continued to speak, haltingly. With this John became enraged and stood up, repeating his previous statement in Spanish. The Russian man's tone of voice became apologetic as looked at the rest of us sheepishly. I shrugged my shoulders indicating I did not understand John's attitude. John continued to yell at and berate the man.

I interrupted, offering, "Maybe he doesn't understand you."

But John responded, " He knows what I am saying!"

Finally the Russian walked away in confusion. When I asked what he had done to warrant this treatment, John snapped, "I caught the commie goin' through the cupboards in the lounge!" But everyone knew the lounge was open and the cupboards contained nothing of value. The party dispersed soon after with everyone feeling a bit uncomfortable.

What would be the best explanation for John's behavior toward the Russian man?

Options

1. Americans and Mexicans are private oriented, as opposed to Russians who are communal, and seeing the Russian man looking through something that didn't belong to him violated this norm.
2. Anti-Russian propaganda in the U.S. has fostered a hatred and distrust of Russians, and John was influenced by this.
3. John's lack of understanding of the Russian man and his culture frustrated him, causing him to become angry.
4. John believed the Russian man was violating the Russian system of in/out groups by approaching the circle and felt inclined to keep him out.

Analysis of Options

1. This is a good choice, and undoubtedly played a part in the situation, but doesn't explain the extent of the incident.
2. Although the U.S. does promote negative feelings toward Russia, and John did draw from this, alone it doesn't cover this incident.

3. This is the best answer; ignorance and intolerance seemed to play the starring role in John's anger. While John claimed the Russian man understood his words and norms, he obviously did not, leading to this confrontation.
4. There is no indication this is a motivating factor in this case.

78

Rachel and her family traveled from California to Connecticut for six weeks one summer to visit some relatives. A few weeks into her vacation Rachel was laying by the pool and listening to some music that was popular with people in her age group in California, and her uncle, Bruce, walked by her and told her to turn that "nigger shit" off. Coming from an extremely culturally diverse area of the country, Rachel didn't understand what made her uncle so upset that she was playing music by a person that he assumed was an African American. The music was what most U.S. Americans would call rhythm and blues, or some might also categorize it as pop music. The artist singing the song was not an African American. Seeing that her uncle was serious, Rachel didn't ask any questions, she just turned the radio off and lay there quietly until her uncle walked away. Rachel was uneasy around her relatives during the rest of her vacation.

Why was Rachel so surprised and why was Bruce so upset over a song?

Options

1. Bruce was stereotyping and judging something that he knew nothing about.
2. Bruce didn't like pop music.
3. Rachel was being rude for playing her music so loud.

Analysis of Options

1. This is the best answer. Bruce was raised in a small town in Connecticut where everyone around him was Caucasian. He was taught to be prejudiced against others and he was stereotyping pop music as music that only African Americans sing, so he assumed that if the singer sang pop, she must be an African American. He didn't think it was appropriate for Rachel to be listening to music that an African American person sang.
2. There is no indication of this in the story. We can assume that Bruce doesn't like pop music because he stereotypes Pop as an African person's music, but this isn't clear in the story.
3. Rachel's uncle was not angered by the volume of the music but by the content of it. There was no mention of the music being too loud. Please try again.

79

Sheri, who is a nurse on an orthopedics unit, was in charge of a patient who was admitted for lower back pain. She was a pleasant enough 25-year-old female, who needed something every 5–10 minutes: pillow puffing, face rinsing, hair brushing, sheet straightening, drape pulling and phone answering. After five hours of constant care Sheri returned to the nurses station only to find the patient's call light on again. To this Sheri exclaimed, "Not again, can't do enough fast enough for her." In response the chief resident asked, "Is she a JAP?" To this Sheri rebutted, " No, she's Caucasian." With that the entire nurses station exploded in hysterical laughter. Sheri left, embarrassed and confused, to see what her patient needed.

Why did they laugh at Sheri?

Options

1. It was late in the P.M. shift and everyone was punchy.
2. Because it wasn't hospital policy to admit the Japanese.
3. Sheri treated all patients as equals and was unfamiliar with slang.
4. They really didn't care about Sheri's problems.

Analysis of Options

1. Even though it was getting late it wasn't a very busy evening except for Sheri. Choose again.
2. Choose again, hospitals admit all patients.
3. This is the correct response. Sheri was unfamiliar to the term JAP, Jewish American Princess, an obviously negative term.
4. This isn't the best answer because people who work in health care generally are there to help each other.

80

My story takes place on a balmy March afternoon in East Los Angeles at approximately 3:30 P.M. While on tour with the De Anza College touring bands, I and three of my fellow musicians entered a Taco Bell in the neighboring vicinity of UCLA. While standing in line and reading the menu, my friends and I were discussing why the bean burrito costs more than the soft taco. I pontificated that beans cost more to slaughter than cows.

Listening in on our conversation were two Hispanic male adults. At this point my Hispanic counterparts displayed a high degree of verbal hostility to my statement. The verbal assaults followed by the fortification of Hispanic peers continued into the dining area, and tensions reached a critical point.

Why did these men become hostile?

Options

1. An incident had previously occurred which had agitated the Hispanic men.
2. A potential language barrier prevented an understanding of the context of my statement.
3. They were merely looking to be provoked into a physical confrontation.
4. They perceived the term "slaughter beans" as a racial epithet endorsing the killing of "beaners."

Analysis of Options

1. This is possible but unlikely due to their pleasant demeanor upon entering.
2. This is likely because their verbal assaults were mostly in Spanish. Once I explained the entire conversation, we were able to shake hands and enjoy a peaceful meal.
3. This solution would define less than mature reasoning capabilities for these individuals and is unlikely.
4. This is an apparent solution. However, since beans were on the menu, this misunderstanding is unlikely.

81

The high school I attended was 45% Latinos. I was a senior in high school; it was getting close to graduation day, and many of us seniors were getting anxious. The person in charge of the graduation ceremony was our new vice principal, Mr. Smith. Before the actual graduation ceremony we had to practice it a couple of times to make sure that everything went right. So by the end of the practice, many of us were getting very nervous.

Some of us Chicano students decided to wear the colors of the Mexican flag, because many other cultures were going to represent theirs. Mr. Smith said that only certain students were allowed to represent their culture. Many of us were upset that we were not allowed to wear what we thought was an appropriate way to represent our culture, so we confronted Mr. Smith after the practice and were expressing our thoughts. Mr. Smith would still not allow us to represent our culture. Consequently, the students began to argue and left angry at him.

What was the cause for the students to feel angry?

Options

1. The students just wanted to get attention.
2. Some of the students wanted to be heard for once.
3. The students felt that their culture could be represented symbolically by the Mexican flag colors.
4. The students felt they were being discriminated against.

Analysis of Options

1. The incident mentions that they might want to show their culture, but not in the sense to get attention from others. Try again.
2. It seems highly unlikely that the students were rebelling, and they just wanted to be heard.
3. The students believed this was an effective way to represent their culture, and were unhappy that someone would tell them otherwise. This is a possibility, but there is a better answer.
4. The students were correct because some students were allowed to represent their culture and others were not. All should have been allowed to represent their cultures equally. This is the best answer.

82

Starting in the seventh grade, my junior high school had the policy of introducing students to several foreign languages. I subsequently took a quarter semester in French, German, and Spanish. Since students in my school system were required to take at least two years in a foreign language, these introductory courses were designed to help students select a language based on prior experience. I decided to take a full semester of German.

I found the culture surrounding the German language fascinating. I also had heard that the English language has its roots in German, so I thought taking German would be easier than any of the other choices. Unfortunately, my mother was not overjoyed in my choice for a foreign language. You see, my mother is Jewish.

All I ever wanted was for my mother to be proud of me. When I would recite my "dialogs" to her, all I wanted was for her to be impressed with how well I was leaning the language. I could tell my mother did not like me speaking German around her, and at some point I stopped involving her in my studies. I eventually completed five years of German, but I always knew my mother did not approve of my choice, as it was this choice that often was the source of great tension in our relationship.

Why did it bother my mother that I was learning a foreign language?

Options

1. She felt that learning Spanish would be more practical.
2. She wanted me to spend more time mowing the lawn and less time studying.
3. She didn't understand the Sapir-Whorf Hypothesis.
4. My mother has negative opinions about Germany and the German language.

Analysis of Options

1. This is not a likely choice. I suspect that my mother would have preferred that I had selected French, but the real issue here is understanding why my mother has such distaste for anything German.
2. The lawn was always well maintained. Choose again.
3. This incident has nothing to do with the Sapir-Whorf Hypothesis. Move on.
4. This is the best response. My mother was born in 1930, and grew up during the depression and World War II. She would occasionally tell me that she knew people who had died in German concentration camps. She also knew people who had managed to survive the Holocaust, but still bore the scars of the experience, both internally and externally, emotionally and physically. For many Jewish people, the German language serves as the antecedent of contact that influences their interactions. My mother was unable to share in my fascination of German culture, since she was inclined to see German culture in terms of anti-Semitism culminating in the desire to exterminate the Jewish race. I knew this was why my mother disliked my studying the German language, but I was hoping that she could understand that all things German do not have to do with Hitler. Unfortunately, her ethnic history is simply too much a part of her cultural identity for her to dismiss what happened to over six million people.

83

I spent the first twenty-one years of my life living in southeastern Pennsylvania. When I was twenty-one, I joined the military. During the four years I was in the military, I met literally thousands of people from all parts of the world and specifically the United States. One group of people was particularly memorable. These people were from the "South."

Frankly, I never though of myself as a "Yankee" growing up in the "North." I also didn't give much thought about the United States Civil War. The Civil War was something I read about in history books. It happened, it's over, case closed. Unfortunately, some people I met while I was still in the military still thought very much in terms of North and South.

I remember several guys telling me that "the South shall rise again," or they would only marry a Southern girl, or they would condescendingly call me a Yankee. I always found such behavior strange, as I never thought of myself as a Yankee or that people from the South were rebels. I also didn't see how a Southern girl was any different from a Northern girl. As for the "South shall rise again," I thought it had risen!

Why are some people still obsessed over the United States Civil War?

Options
1. Some people cannot accept the fact that the South lost the war.
2. Some people would like to see the return of slavery.
3. People in the South are afraid of Northerners.
4. People in the South have a unique cultural group history and identity.

Analysis of Options
1. There may be some truth to this option, but it's doubtful. Try again.
2. No way! Some of the people who voiced such pro-South positions were African-American, making this option unlikely.
3. I never detected fear as being the basis for such pro-Southern sentiment. Sometimes fear is the basis for prejudice, but in this case I don't believe this is true.
4. This is the best choice. While the civil war was a unifying force for the nation, the South still maintains its own culture. The history of the Civil War is very much today a part of the culture for *some* people who live in the South. Also, people get their identity through their history. Since it was the South that lost the war, some people in the South carry with them the identity of the people who were forced to join with the North. It is this forced joining to the North that makes some people from the South want to remain separate, even if it is in their own private way. Somebody did point out to me that people from the South who talk about North/South issues along with the civil war, are most likely uneducated. Since many people who join the military are from a lower social and/or economic class, it is not surprising that the people who refer to people as Yankees are uneducated. It is important to understand that such people do carry with them their own culture, based on their history and identity, and it is their history and identity that helps explain their attitudes toward people from other geographical regions of the country.

84

In 1991, my husband and I had dinner in Monterey, California. The waitress seated us at a table placed next to a wall mirror. My husband and I could observe anyone they seated next to us. Shortly, after they served us our hors d'oeuvres, I excused myself to go to the restroom. Upon my return they had seated a white South African family to our left. The adult man was staring at me as I approached my table. My husband, who is an African American, said the man had been staring at him since their arrival. I am European American and I felt self-conscious. The family was seated close enough to us that we overheard their conversation. The mother was discussing what to order for dinner with her children while the husband continued to stare at us. The mother and children were fidgeting in their chairs, and there were long gaps in their conversation. The staring lasted through our main course and dessert. Eventually the wife asked her husband to please stop staring and pay attention to their supper. The man was staring so hard at us, he almost missed his mouth when he lifted his fork to it. Eric and I tried shutting all of this out, but it was impossible—the man's face was plastered in our wall mirror. Eric and I were feeling uncomfortable and were relieved when the dinner was over.

Why was this man staring so blatantly?

Options

1. South Africans are accustomed to staring at each other during dinner.
2. South Africans are curious about cultures different than their own.
3. Eric and I were being overly self-conscious as to the amount of attention we were getting.
4. White South Africans are not accustomed to dining in the same restaurant as black people or interracial couples.

Analysis of Options

1. No, this is incorrect. There is a better solution. It is considered rude to stare at people for long lengths of time, even in South Africa.
2. This may be some consolation, and my validation sample found this possible, but it was not very convincing to Eric and I. There are factors involving our reaction to the attention we received that have more validity.
3. Although there may be some element of truth in this, it is not customary to stare at other people for long lengths of time.
4. This is the best solution. In 1991, black South Africans were considered third class citizens by most white South Africans. Furthermore, interracial couples are not a social norm in South Africa. I felt this man and his family were ill prepared for U.S. American culture. They should have expected to see equal treatment between blacks and whites.

85

work with people from different countries everyday. With people from different cultures coming from a different business environment, it is very easy to have misunderstandings and misinterpretations. Most of the time, a person involved in a misunderstanding can just ask the other person to clarify himself. However, there are certain taboo subjects that some people do not wish to clarify, but just want to forget.

Such a situation occurred at work with me and this man named Guido. Guido is a thirty-seven-year-old, single man from Italy. Sometimes, when Guido and I are speaking, my defense signals go off. I wonder if Guido is making advances toward me. For example, I was folding promotional shirts for our center, and I commented on how all the shirts came only in X-large. In response, Guido made a comment about how I could wear that only as a dress, and that would be very "sexy."

I have been brought up in the United States where that kind of comment in the workplace is not socially acceptable. I get confused sometimes by the mannerisms of some Italian and Brazilian men. Sometimes when I see Guido during a social visit, he will give me a kiss on both cheeks. I entertain his customs to an extent; however, there is a line that I will not allow to be crossed.

What would help me understand these situations better?

Options

1. Italian cultures differ from American cultures by personal space and public display of affection.
2. Guido is a dirty, old man who is taking advantage of another person because she thinks it is part of his culture.
3. Guido feels comfortable in his actions because I make no effort to tell him that his actions make me uncomfortable.
4. All factors (1 through 3) play a part.

Analysis of Options

1. Option one seems likely in some of my past experiences; a lot, but not all, of Italians seem to have less of a personal space distance and are more physically affectionate with friends.
2. Unfortunately, I think Guido is a little bit of a "dirty old man." He realizes that I am a young, tolerating person and that he is a single man from a different country. He might try to see how far he can go with those facts.
3. Option three is very true. Since I don't want to make any ripples in the company, I don't tell him that his actions make me uncomfortable. Doing so might help him understand why I back away when he comes near me.
4. Option four is probably the most accurate. I recognize the factors that I could deal with if I had the guts. If I took into account cultural differences and individual concerns, maybe I could work out a solution that makes both Guido and myself feel comfortable.

86

One day at work, Steven (who is white) saw his coworker Kevin (who is African-American), and went over to chat. Steven noticed that Kevin was wearing a T-shirt with a nude female on it. Steven made an off hand comment that he felt this sort of T-shirt was not entirely appropriate for the workplace. Kevin replied that the female was depicting an African dance and didn't say anything else. For the next several days, Steven noticed that Kevin was very difficult to get along with. Kevin's general attitude seemed to change.

Why was Kevin upset?

Options

1.   He didn't like having his choice in clothes criticized.
2.   Since Steven was not his superior, Kevin felt that what he wore was none of Steven's business.
3.   Kevin took Steven's comment as an affront on his culture, and felt that Steven's insensitivity was typical of the way whites treat African-Americans in general.
4.   The nude female on Kevin's shirt was his mother and he interpreted Steven's comment as an insult against his mother.

Analysis of Options

1.   This is possible, but unlikely.
2.   This is certainly a possibility but it doesn't quite fit the situation. Choose again.
3.   This is the best choice. Even though racial and cultural discrimination is for the most part illegal and continues to decline, minorities still endure a lot of prejudice. There are still people that believe that other people, because of their cultural backgrounds, are second class citizens and treat them accordingly. Further, there is much debate between whites and African Americans about the amount of prejudice still practiced. Many whites feel that prejudice is under control and declining. Many African-Americans feel that injustice is on the rise. To Kevin, Steven came across just like other prejudiced whites he had encountered.
4.   This option is very unlikely.

After a few days Steven figured out that Kevin's change in behavior started after the T-shirt comment. After thinking about it, Steven realized that he had not communicated himself very well and that his comment could have been interpreted as being racist. Steven immediately met with Kevin to explain that his comment was not in any way intended to be anti African-American and apologized for not choosing his words more carefully. Steven explained that he initially interpreted Kevin's T-shirt as being like the Playboy calendars the building maintenance guys had posted in their shop. These calendars and posters are offensive to the female workers at the company and the company was beginning a program to educate the male workers and get the male workers to remove their calendars and posters. Kevin accepted Steven's apology. Kevin's attitude and work ethic improved so much after his talk with Steven that six months later he was promoted.

87

BC," which stands for American Born Chinese, is a term widely used among Chinese here in America. Most first generation Chinese here don't consider ABC as "real Chinese." Although they may look Chinese, they are no different from Americans in the way they talk, act, dress, etc.

Sam, a good friend of mine, is an ABC. Although Sam's parents are Chinese, they both barely know how to speak Chinese, so basically Sam is not very accustomed to Chinese culture.

My parents were going to bring me to the Chinese New Year event in our local Chinese community. Chinese gathered together to celebrate the New Year. I told Sam about it. Being outgoing and social, he was excited to attend the event. On the day of the event, my parents and I were a little late. As I walked to the door, I saw Sam coming out in a black suit. "Hi, Sam. Where are you going?" I was aware of the unhappy look on Sam's face. He shrugged his shoulders.

"Going home."

"Why? Didn't you just get here?" I asked.

"Because," he replied, "I think people in there are rude."

"Rude?" I was rather surprised.

"Yeah, after I went in, everybody started looking at me in a weird way, like I did something wrong, and everybody seemed to be trying to avoid me or something."

What happened to Sam?

Options

1. Sam arrived too early.
2. Sam wore the wrong color.
3. Sam should not have attended the event alone.
4. Sam should have brought a gift.

Analysis of Options

1. This is not correct. The story indicates there were other people at the celebration already.
2. This is the best answer. In Chinese culture, one should wear something in a bright color on the day of the Chinese New Year for auspiciousness. Some traditional Chinese believe that wearing black at Chinese New Year brings bad luck for the whole year, and so is disrespectful to the people around you. In Sam's case, the solution is quite simple—change the outfit.
3. Although it would have been easier for Sam to attend the event with someone who was more familiar with the community, this factor alone does not explain the others' reactions.
4. This is incorrect. My family did not bring gifts either.

88

I started the nursing program here at De Anza College last quarter. Right now I am into my second quarter of the program and I really love it. There is a great mixture of different ethnicities in my nursing group and everyone seems to get along fine. Within our group of twenty-two, there are about four or five different cliques. I always see this happening in any class I have had. I believe this occurs because you tend to stay with the people that you identify with the most.

Our clinical rotations are always at different hospitals, and this quarter, we are at a hospital in Redwood City. There was an incident that occurred that really bothered me. It involved my classmate Christine, who is Caucasian, and myself, being Filipino. We were both assigned to the same nurse, Laura, who was also Caucasian. I then introduced myself to Laura and explained to her who I was and who I would be working with. She did not really say anything in return. Throughout my shift, I would ask her questions if I needed help or some clarification. Laura seemed very reluctant to assist me and not receptive to any of my questions. I kept thinking to myself, "Am I doing something wrong?" On the other hand, every time I heard her with Christine, she was explaining everything to her and even offered her assistance if she needed it. I just could not understand what the problem was.

Why did Laura respond to me the way she did?

Options

1. Laura was having a bad day and just took it out on me because she felt like it.
2. She thought I was asking her too many questions and was irritated with me.
3. She did not have the patience to deal with both Christine and me.
4. She had a bad experience with Filipino student nurses.

Analysis of Options

1. This response is unlikely because she did not treat Christine that way and anyone else that I could observe.
2. This is probably the best answer because I was asking her quite a few questions throughout my shift and I could have asked one of the other nurses or my instructor to assist me.
3. This is a possible answer because maybe Laura only wanted one student nurse assigned to her and she felt more comfortable with Christine.
4. This is also unlikely because I would never know if she ever had a bad experience with Filipino students. I may have just been a person she could not identify with.

89

About six years ago my co-workers and I were taking a break and reflecting about our manager who liked being referred to as "Rambo." He had a son who, although was white, was known as "Buckwheat." As we were talking about these two individuals, a fairly good friend of mine, Dwight, who is black, said he would not want to be called "Rambo." I started laughing and quipped, "Dwight, they wouldn't call you Rambo, they would call you Sambo."

He remarked, "I don't play that game," and I tried to explain that I was joking. I had known Dwight for 11 years before this incident. We had socialized on a regular basis and supported each other through difficult events. Dwight even told another black inspector about the incident and she replied, "Susie didn't mean anything by that, she must have been joking."

Trying to resolve any bad feelings, I went to my boss and explained the situation. I wanted to have a meeting with Dwight to apologize. But nothing was ever resolved and I still feel bad. Every time I see Dwight I am on guard about everything I say or do.

How could I resolve this situation?

Options

1. Get together over a drink and apologize.
2. Offer to do anything or talk to anyone else that was offended.
3. Move on, and in future conversations try to be sensitive in content as to not offend others.
4. Tell Dwight he's too sensitive.

Analysis of Options

1. This is a possibility. I tried meeting with Dwight to apologize before and it didn't work. But my persistence might demonstrate my sincerity, and the passage of time may have diminished Dwight's anger.
2. This is a nice gesture, but will probably not resolve the situation because it does not deal with Dwight's feelings specifically. Also, the incident does not mention others being offended.
3. This is also a possibility. Clearly Dwight was offended enough by the remark to end a strong friendship. He might consider that type of behavior over the line and not worth forgiving. However, it is impossible to know that without asking Dwight directly.
4. This is the worst possible action. Choose again.

90

For all of my life I have been considered a Pacific Islander, through school systems, ethnic surveys, and daily background groupings, but I always told everyone I was Hawaiian. That's where I am from and that is the culture that I identify with. One day I was in the gym at school just playing basketball and the substitute for our class came up to me and started talking to me. I had no problem with this and I was quite honored, because he didn't know me and was talking to me like he had known me for years. We talked about school, what I wanted to do in the future, what my major was, and many other things. He had asked if I played any sports for my school, and I answered him honestly, "No." Well, out of the blue he asked if I was Hawaiian. And I said, "Yes, why do you ask?" He just said because I was wearing a Hawaiian strength T-shirt. I said, "Yes, I am Hawaiian and very proud of my culture."

Later on in the conversation he said that I must be Samoan or Tongan, and wanted to know which one I was. I kind of just shook my head and was sort of quiet. I really didn't know what else to say. Then I told him, "No, I am just Hawaiian." I tried to move to a different court and stay away. He just kept following me and talking to me but I really didn't want him around. It's like he didn't understand what was wrong with this picture.

Why was this student upset?

Options

1. She was just tired of listening to him about all of his random topics.
2. She was offended that he had assumed that she was Samoan or Tongan just because she was Hawaiian.
3. She has short tolerances for closed-minded individuals.
4. She wanted to concentrate on her basketball skills and he was taking up too much of her time.

Analysis of Options

1. Although many people would get annoyed with a person constantly talking to them while they are trying to play basketball, this is logically not the reason for this student suddenly becoming quiet. In society there are many people that not only talk too much but have a very outgoing personality and that is probably what he had.
2. This is the best answer. Although she was comfortable with him at first because he was talking to her like they had known each other for years, the relationship was affected tremendously when one person didn't know enough about the other culture. In the Hawaiian culture the people, when meeting each other for the first time, usually feel very comfortable and when involved in a conversation can talk for hours as if they had known each other for years. With that, this student felt comfortable with him. However, later on he violated the relationship by assuming that she was Samoan or Tongan. He had thought that in the Hawaiian Islands if you were from there you were either of Samoan or Tongan ethnic background. Since she was offended by the remark, it made her uncomfortable with him and that is what made her keep quiet and try to move to another court.
3. Although she probably did get a little temperamental with the substitute because of his prejudging, it was not the main focus on why she had suddenly gotten quiet and wanted to move to a different court. The assumption that he made had offended her but not enough to make her feel as if he was an offensive, closed-minded individual. It was just all the people that he had ever known to be Hawaiian also had Samoan and/or Tongan in them.

4. This is definitely not the answer. Yes, she was playing basketball and working on her skills, but him talking to her was not the reason for her to keep quiet. She could definitely do more than one thing at a time. Please choose again.

91

I work in a small bagel shop in Mountain View in a large shopping center. At times we get extremely busy with a line forming outside the door, and with only two servers it can get confusing when it comes to who's next in line. My usual call to organize some of the chaos is, "Can I help the next person?" It usually works, but not today. I called for the next person in line and a young woman stepped forward and gave me her order. I helped her, did the money thing, and she was on her way. I again called for the next person when another woman stepped forward to give her order and a man standing next to her gave out a large sigh.

"I'm sorry were you next?" I asked apologetically.

"Yes, I was," he exclaimed angrily.

"Okay, can I help you?"

"Never mind now," he stated forcefully and stormed out the door.

About an hour later the baker approached me and told me that someone had called to complain about me. The man on the phone wanted to speak to the owner of the store and proceeded to explain that he was going to call the Better Business Bureau because I was being racist and discriminatory due to his being Asian.

How was this situation taken the wrong way?

Options

1. He was put in a bad mood due to a prior incident that day.
2. I was in the wrong and should have known he was next.
3. He believes people see him only by his race.
4. I did ignore him because of his race.

Analysis of Options

1. There is a possibly that someone had discriminated against him because of his race earlier that day or he was just having a bad day and this incident pushed him over the edge. But he was quite sure I was being racist. Please choose again.
2. The only way to truly keep track of who is next is to have a take a number system to make sure everyone is in the right order. However, this is not my decision to make. As mentioned in the incident, it is sometimes very difficult to keep track of the order of the customers. In this system, we use the honor system and are reliant on the customers to tell us who is next. There is a better answer.
3. This is the best answer. It is very likely this man has been discriminated against frequently in the past. Therefore, he incorrectly assumes every action directed toward him is based on discriminatory motives. He is guilty of fundamental attribution error.
4. I do not believe I am racist or discriminatory, and I do not believe one could infer this about me by this incident alone. Also he has no idea who I am or what I believe and to be called racist and discriminatory are pretty strong words when you don't even have a full conversation with someone. Please choose again.

92

I had only been in the U.S. for two months as a student from France when I met Nikkos at a party on a Friday evening. He was from Greece where he had lived until he was 20 years old and then came to the U.S. to go to college. He had been living in the U.S. for 10 years when I met him. Not having friends, since I had just recently relocated from France, I accepted Nikkos' invitation to visit San Francisco with him the following weekend.

From the beginning of our visit, he was very friendly and gallant. He opened the door of the car for me. He took me to the Hard Rock Cafe and then we were having a wonderful time walking at the Wharf, Pier 39, and Coit Tower, when Nikkos insisted on buying me a sweater with the inscription "San Francisco" on it. I was very surprised by his offer and I refused to accept it, telling him that if I wanted a sweater, I could buy it myself! He insisted again telling me how he would be very happy to offer me this sweater. I was so upset by his persistence that I lied to him and told him that I already had a sweater from San Francisco. Nikkos accepted my answer and as if nothing had happened, he took me to visit the Golden Gate Bridge. When I slipped on a rock and almost fell, he tried to hold my hand, which I coldly withdrew. After our visit, Nikkos brought me home and told me that he would call me the next day. I never called him and never returned his phone calls.

What could be the cause of this misunderstanding?

Options

1. I was not feeling comfortable with Nikkos because I had met him only one time before that day.
2. I thought that Nikkos felt obligated to buy me the sweater because I didn't have a lot of money.
3. I thought that Nikkos was trying to take advantage of me by buying me a present.
4. I didn't want Nikkos to think that our relationship could become more serious.

Analysis of Options

1. I was not feeling as comfortable as I usually am with somebody that I know well, but being new in this country I was ready to make friends and forget about my shyness. Please choose again.
2. I had never told Nikkos that I was interested in the sweater. He had seen it outside of a store and decided to offer it to me. Consequently, even though he knew that I was a student and didn't have too much money, he didn't have reasons to feel obligated to buy me this sweater.
3. This is the right answer. In French culture, when a man invites a woman for a first date, he is not supposed to offer any presents to the woman. This is perceived by the woman as a gesture to get the woman's favors. When Nikkos offered to buy me this sweater, I felt that he was doing this because he was expecting me to have a sexual relationship with him in return. Thinking that way, I perceived his help when I slipped on the rock as another of his efforts to get something from me. Nikkos was Greek and in his culture it is normal for a man to pay when he invites a woman for a date. The contrary would be considered as being rude and not gallant. Also in this case, Nikkos wanted to buy me a sweater with the inscription "San Francisco" which can be remembered as a souvenir.
4. This is not the answer. When I accepted Nikkos' invitation, I was not against an eventual serious relationship between us. At the beginning of our visit, I liked him very much as a friend and I was really nicely surprised by his gallantry and kindness.

Comments

These incidents present us with good examples of how cultures differ in their expectations for behavior within a *social context*. A social context is any opportunity for intercultural interaction in which both parties are unfamiliar with one another. This may occur at the market, at work, in a classroom, at a party, or on a first date. Every culture has its own *norms*, or rules for behavior within particular contexts (Shimanoff, 1980). Therefore, when people are from different cultures, we can see that even the simplest norm can cause great misunderstanding. For example, in incident 92 in our French student's eyes, Nikkos was not following appropriate social norms. He was far too forward in buying gifts and offering to hold hands. These subtle actions indicated to her that he was propositioning her for sex. However, in Nikkos' Greek culture, he was simply engaging in behavior that was expected and considered polite, with no suggestion of "payback" later. Incident 87 also illustrates this concept. Although Sam believed he was polite by dressing up for the Chinese New Year celebration, other members of the community thought he was rude for wearing black.

When people from different cultures misunderstand one another's norms, *fundamental attribution error* often occurs (Ross, 1977). As you recall from Chapter 1, attributions are the judgments that we make about ourselves and others. In particular, when we make attributions about other people that are from cultures different from ours, we often fall into the pitfall of judging those people by our own cultural standards. How can we expect people from other cultures to know our cultural rules? Although this may seem to be a foolish question, this is often how we behave. We make negative judgments about people because they did not follow *our* cultural rules without understanding their cultural rules. This is fundamental attribution error. However, most people do not stop at the judgment because that judgment influences our behavior.

Consequently, fundamental attribution error often transcends into *autistic hostility*. Autistic hostility is unexpressed anger resulting from intercultural misunderstanding. So if we judge someone negatively, we usually decide never to speak to him or her again, as our French student did with Nikkos in incident 92. Obviously, this is not the most effective intercultural communication technique. A better strategy would be to discuss one another's rules and interpretations of behaviors. This way, misunderstanding would be reduced and we would actually learn from each other. We can then, of course, carry that knowledge with us to other intercultural encounters.

One basic reason we fall victim to these problems is because we all *perceive* stimuli differently. Our perceptions of events become our reality (Goffman, 1974). When we experience an event, we all *select, organize,* and *interpret* that event differently. In other words, our culture, among other factors, influences what we decide to pay attention to, how we relate that information to other aspects of our lives, and how we make sense of those events. R. D. Laing (1966) explains that our perceptions will influence our actions. If we perceive an event in a particular way, then we are going to behave accordingly, not realizing that our interpretation may be incorrect. This problem is illustrated in incident 89 when Dwight misinterpreted his friend's comment. He interpreted the "Sambo" comment based on past experiences with discrimination and prejudice, whereas his friend interpreted the comment based on the strong friendship the two men enjoyed.

While the perception process is universal (everyone does it), if we organize and interpret events too rigidly, we may commit the error of *stereotyping*. Stereotyping is a selection process that simplifies our perceptions of others and leads to generalizations about a group of people; they are inaccurate, rigid, and inflexible characterizations of people that overlook positive or negative attributes (Lippmann, 1922). When we stereotype, we do not see people as individuals, but rather as categories, as in incidents 69, 71, 77, and 78.

One common way to stereotype is through *stigmatized speech*. We form perceptions about people through their speaking style or language. If someone speaks similarly to our own style, we tend to judge that person positively, assuming that person belongs to the same group as us. However, if someone speaks differently from our style, we know that person belongs to a different group and frequently judge that person negatively because of it. We can see this phenomena occurring in incidents 73 and 74.

Clearly, stereotyping quickly becomes an obstacle to communication. Stereotyping often leads to *prejudice* and *discrimination*. Prejudice is a negative reaction to people based upon inaccurate and rigid stereotypes and discrimination is the behavioral manifestation of prejudice, in other words prejudice in action (Lustig & Koester, 1999). Hence, our perceptions, stereotypes, and prejudices influence how we behave toward other people, as illustrated in incident 84. In the case of discrimination, this behavior is usually negative and intended to put the receiver of the discrimination at a disadvantage.

Additionally, *history* plays a large part in our reactions toward others. According to Brislin (1981), parts of our history influence how we interact with people in the present. Childhood experiences, historical myths, languages, and recent events are such factors. Additionally, one's past experiences or one's ancestor's past experiences will also influence behavior toward others. For example, if one's parents teach that person to hate others from a particular culture, he or she may become racist as an adult. Or if one person's culture has been discriminated against in the past (i.e., Holocaust), those people may be wary of the cultural group that did the discriminating (i.e., Germans). Or if one experiences discrimination frequently from a random number of people, that person may assume that everyone discriminates. We can see these factors at work in incidents 72, 82, 83, 88, and 91, among others.

Thus, there are many variables that make communication more difficult and understanding less likely, and critical incidents like these are difficult to make sense of while we are experiencing them. If we can remember these concepts and try to apply them, though, we will eventually be able to practice intercultural communication in a more competent manner.

Judgment Exercises

Exercise 1. D. I. E.

Look at the picture presented on the next page. Use the D.I.E. Framework as discussed in class to analyze the situation and complete the form below.

DESCRIPTION

_____
_____
_____
_____
_____
_____
_____
_____
_____

INTERPRETATIONS

_____
_____
_____
_____
_____
_____
_____
_____
_____
_____

EVALUATION

_____
_____
_____
_____
_____
_____
_____
_____
_____
_____

Copyright by Anti-Defamation League Rumor Clinic. Reprinted by permission.

Exercise 2. Perception Checking

Perception checking is a great tool to help you understand others and express yourself clearly. It is an aid to communicating effectively because it is clear, honest, and not judgmental. More importantly, it serves to help communication partners to understand other's perceptions as well as their own.

To perception check, follow these three steps:

1. **Describe the event as objectively as possible.**
2. **Explain at least two possible interpretations of that event.**
3. **Ask for clarification.**

You've been quiet all afternoon. Are you not feeling well or did something happen at school? Let's talk for a minute.

You walked right past me without saying hello. It makes me curious if you're mad at me or just in a hurry. How are you feeling?

In groups of four, practice responding to the following scenarios with perception checking statements. Use this opportunity to critique each other and to offer alternative responses.

Scenario One

Your manager at work speaks in a condescending style. While you know he/she is not singling you out (it happens with everybody), it does bother you and distracts you from your work as you stew about it.

Perception Checking Statement:

_____

_____

_____

_____

_____

Scenario Two

A coworker of yours always wants to gossip and play around when the boss is not looking. You enjoy working with this person, but you also need to meet some goals for a promotion.

Perception Checking Statement:

_____

_____

_____

_____

_____

Scenario Three

You have a friend who calls and comes by to see you often. This person is always depressed and wants to spend hours discussing his/her problems with you, never giving you the chance to discuss your own life. You want to help your friend, but you are beginning to feel like a therapist!

Perception Checking Statement:

_____

_____

_____

_____

_____

Scenario Four

Your significant other says he/she wants to support you through school, but also gets upset when you need to study instead of spending "fun" time with him/her. You feel torn in two.

Perception Checking Statement:

_____

_____

_____

_____

_____

Exercise 3. Stereotypes and the Media

Describe five stereotypes you have found in the mass media: television, radio, newspapers, magazines, Internet, etc.

Stereotype 1: _____
_____
_____

Stereotype 2: _____
_____
_____

Stereotype 3: _____
_____
_____

Stereotype 4: _____
_____
_____

Stereotype 5: _____
_____
_____

Exercise 4. Personal Assessment Questions

A. What stereotypes are you familiar with? How do you think they developed? How might they influence communication?

_____

_____

_____

_____

_____

_____

_____

_____

_____

_____

B. Describe your experiences with discrimination.

_____

_____

_____

_____

_____

_____

_____

_____

_____

_____

C. What historical forces have influenced how you see the world or how you communicate?

_____

_____

_____

_____

_____

_____

_____

_____

_____

_____

_____

Exercise 5. Cultural Partner Question

Your cultural partner may have had some stereotypes about the community you both live in now. Ask your partner to describe those stereotypes. Why did your partner form those stereotypes? Were any reinforced or repudiated?

References

Adler, R. B. and Towne, N. (1999). Looking out/looking in: Interpersonal Communication, 9th ed. Fort Worth: Harcourt Brace.

Argyle, M. and Dean, J. (1965). *Eye-contact, distance, and affiliation* in Sociometry 28, 289–304.

Berger, C. and Calabrese, R. (1975). *Some explorations in initial interaction and beyond.* Human communication research, 1, 99–112.

Brislin, R. W. (1981). Cross cultural encounters: Face to face interaction. New York: Pergamon.

Cushner, K. and Brislin, R. W. (1996). Intercultural interactions: A practical guide, 2nd ed. Thousand Oaks: Sage.

Goffman, E. (1974). Frame analysis: An essay on the organization of experience. Cambridge: Harvard University Press.

Hall, E. T. (1959) The silent language. New York: Doubleday.

Hall, E. T. (1976). Beyond culture. New York: Doubleday.

Laing, R. D., Phillipson, H., and Lee, A. R. (1966). Interpersonal perception. New York: Springer.

Lippmann, W. (1922). Public opinion. New York: Harcourt, Brace.

Lustig, M. W., and Koester, J. (1999). Intercultural competence: Interpersonal communication across cultures. New York: Longman.

Martin, J. N. and Nakayama, T. K. (2000). Intercultural Communication in Contexts, 2nd ed. Mountain View, CA: Mayfield.

Moghaddam, F., Ditto, B., and Taylor, D. (1990). *Attitudes and attributions related to psychological symptomatology in Indian immigrant women.* Journal of cross-cultural psychology, 21, 335-50.

Oberg, Kalvero. (1960). *Cultural shock: Adjustment to new cultural environments.* Practical Anthropology, 7, 176.

Ogden, C. K. and Richards, I. A. (1923). The meaning of meaning. New York: Harcourt, Brace.

Ross, L. (1977). *The intuitive psychologist and his shortcomings: Distortion in the attribution process.* In L. Berkowitz (Ed.), Advances in experimental social psychology (Vol. 10). New York: Academic Press.

Shimanoff, S. B. (1980). Communication rules: Theory and research. Beverly Hills: Sage.

Triandis, H. C. (1988). *Collectivism vs. individualism.* In G. Verma & C. Bagley (Eds.), Cross-cultural studies of personality, attitudes, and cognition. London: Macmillan.

Wendt, J. (1984). *D.I.E.: A way to improve communication.* Communication Education, 33, 397–401.

Wolvin, A. and Coakley, C. G. (1996). Listening, 5th ed. Madison: Brown and Benchmark.

Appendix: Instructor's Notes

Critical Incidents

The critical incidents comprise the majority of each chapter. If students are reading the incidents on their own, I recommend they use them as self-quizzes, circling the correct "option" before reading the "analysis of options." Of course, the incidents are also useful as supplemental pieces to be read and discussed in the classroom.

I have tried to leave the incidents as close to the original style of the authors, so that as students read them they will relate to them easier. Additionally, many of the "options" and "analysis of options" are solutions provided by intercultural communication students.

Comments

The "comments" section within each chapter is intended to sum up the intercultural communication concepts relevant to that topic area. It also provides an opportunity to discuss the situations in the incidents a little further. The "comments" are not a complete discussion of the topic and are not intended as a replacement to a traditional communication text. Rather, they highlight the issues salient to the incidents and would serve as a supplemental review of the material learned from a standard textbook.

Cultural Partner Questions

A cultural partnership is an extraordinary way to help students apply the concepts they are learning to the real world, and many make a friend they never expected in the process. If your college does not offer such a program, it is simple to start. It is simply a pairing of intercultural communication students with ESL students. Students meet for a number of required hours throughout the term (usually 4–8), get to know each other, and sometimes discuss what they are learning.

The questions at the end of each chapter help the students to gain more information about that particular concept from their partner. They also serve as a useful method to check in with students about the progression of their partnerships and to solve logistics problems.

All students being paired up should complete an information sheet to help determine who will make a good match and to help reduce logistics problems. See the following pages for samples of the information sheet and agreement form. Please reproduce as necessary.

Cultural Partners Program Application

Welcome to the Cultural Partners Program. This program will connect you with another student right here on campus so that you can learn about each others' cultures. We will use the following information to pair you up with your partner, so please complete this form as completely, accurately, and neatly as possible. We will do our best to make a match that works for both of you.

My Name: _____ Male [ ] Female [ ]

Age: _____ My Native Country: _____

Is it okay to pair you with someone of the opposite sex?   yes [ ]   no [ ]

The Language I Know Best: _____

Other Languages: _____

Home Phone Number: _____ Best Time to Call: _____

Work Phone Number: _____ Best Time to Call: _____

Email Address: _____

My Instructor's Name: _____

Class: _____ Days/Times: _____

Major: _____

Profession/Job: _____

Hobbies/Interests: _____

Comments for your partner? _____

_____

_____

_____

My Schedule – Check all times that you can possibly meet with your partner.

	Monday	Tuesday	Wednesday	Thursday	Friday	Saturday	Sunday
7:00–9:00	_____	_____	_____	_____	_____	_____	_____
9:00–12:00	_____	_____	_____	_____	_____	_____	_____
12:00–3:00	_____	_____	_____	_____	_____	_____	_____
3:00–5:00	_____	_____	_____	_____	_____	_____	_____
5:00–8:00	_____	_____	_____	_____	_____	_____	_____

Is there anything else that would help us determine your match?

_____

_____

_____

_____

_____

_____

Cultural Partners Agreement

In order to make your cultural partners experience successful, there are a few conditions that you must agree to. If you agree to all the statements below, print your names on the first two lines. Then sign in the appropriate places at the bottom. If you do not agree with the conditions below, you may not participate in this project.

THIS SIGNED AGREEMENT IS DUE: _____

• We, (print both partners' names here) _____
and _____,
agree to try hard to find a time to meet with each other. We know that sometimes it might be hard to arrange meeting times, but we will try our best to schedule meetings at a time that works well for both of us.

• We promise to meet each other for a total of _____ hours throughout the term.

• We promise to return all phone calls or email to our partner within 24 hours after receiving a message.

• We promise to be on time to all our meetings. If we cannot go to a scheduled meeting, we will tell the other partner at least 24 hours in advance that we need to cancel, and we will ask our partner if we can meet on another day.

• We promise to inform our instructors if we have any problems with our partner. We will talk to them immediately if one partner is not returning phone calls or missing appointments, or if there are any other problems.

• We realize that ultimately it is our responsibility to work out any challenges in meeting our partners. If we fail to meet as the project requires, we will lose our partners.

• We agree not to hold _____ (college) or the instructors liable for any mishap related to this project, especially if we meet off campus. (We recommend meeting on campus.)

• Finally, we agree to ask each other a lot of questions, share our knowledge and experience, and have fun!

ESL Student's Signature _____ Date _____

IC Comm Student's Signature _____ Date _____

Adapted from Marcy Betlach, De Anza College, Cupertino, CA

_ Language Activities _

The Rugby/Bowling Challenge

Performance Objective: Students will demonstrate the ability to accommodate the conversational styles of a target culture.

Author: Piper McNulty, De Anza College, Cupertino, California

Essential Materials: Video: Fluent American English Video Series: Part One: Understanding Conversational Styles Around the Globe: "bowling, basketball and rugby." Available from The Seabright Group, Sacramento, CA. (530) 759-0684. Or, any two commercial (non-training) videos depicting a) Mediterranean proactive/high involvement** style and b) Far Eastern receptive/high considerateness** style. VCR and monitor.

* The terms "rugby," "bowling," "high involvement," and "high considerateness" are taken from the Seabright video listed above.

I-A Videos: Show video clips which illustrate the two contrasting styles (proactive and receptive). (If using the Seabright Group video, show just the clips of the two groups of ESL students discussing Alligator River, and a bit of the clips showing the two types of sports, bowling and rugby. About 5 minutes total). Then lead students in the following activities.

I-B Communication Behaviors Demonstrating Each Style (see Students' Materials III-A)

I-D Making the Teams: Divide the class into an even number of teams of 3–7 students each. Pair the teams, and assign each student a Feedback Partner from their paired team (the Feedback Partner will ideally be a student with a somewhat different natural communication style). While the first team is interacting, the Feedback Partners (students in the second team) will be monitoring the interaction and preparing to give one-on-one feedback.

For example: 36 students: 6 teams of 6 students each.

In each pair of teams, students 1 and 7, 2 and 8, 3 and 9 (etc.) are <u>Feedback Partners</u>.

Team A Students	Team B Students
1	7
2	8
3	9
4	10
5	11
6	12

Team C Students	Team D Students
1	7
2	8
3	9
4	10
5	11
6	12

Team E Students	Team F Students
1	7
2	8
3	9
4	10
5	11
6	12

In most classes you will not have an even mix of rugby and bowling players. In this case, those whom you perceive to be towards the middle can be paired with anyone who has placed themselves on either end of the rugby/bowling continuum. You can also look at ethnic heritage to help you determine which students <u>might</u> have experience style switching, or may be more familiar with alternative styles. A quiet Jewish American or Italian American student may have been around many rugby players. An assertive Asian American student may have relatives who demonstrate the bowling style…. Above all, never make an assumption about your own students' natural styles based on their ethnic heritage. Observe them and ask them how they rated themselves. Note that you may never have both an extreme bowler and an extreme rugby player in one class. However, students may self assess as one extreme or the other. Or, students who actually would fall at one or the other end of the continuum may plot themselves towards the middle. Do not question where they have placed themselves. However, it may become clear during student interactions that a student's self perception differs from the way he presents himself in class. Once good rapport has been established, ask the teams to do a bit of peer feedback. Do they agree with teach member's self assessment?

To highlight the advantages of biculturalism and the dangers of stereotyping, you can also have the students plot themselves along an imaginary line from 1 to 10 across the classroom, using peer interaction in a classroom setting as the context. Ask them to take a good look at where their classmates have placed themselves. Then give them a new context: a family gathering (holiday meal) and have them move to the point along the imaginary continuum which demonstrates their conversational style in this context. In a recent class, one of my students was a 2 (rugby style) in the classroom (a self assessment with which most of his classmates concurred) but a self-described 8 (bowling) at home. The student, a Vietnamese American, was quite assertive in the classroom, but was expected to be quiet and harmonious when interacting with older relatives.

I-D Why Bowling before Rugby?

In the 3 monitored conversations in this series of exercises, It is usually best to have your students practice the bowling style before they practice the rugby style. The reason for this is that in most North American group interactions, especially in a classroom context, the dominant style will be closer to "rugby" than "bowling." If students begin the discussion using the rugby style and then are told to switch to "bowling," the conversation sometimes falls flat. Because of the dominance of a more assertive (rugby-like) style among the majority of North Americans, those students who naturally favor the rugby style may demonstrate so much overt frustration and impatience during the "bowling" portion of the interaction, that students who are natural "bowlers" may feel embarrassed and reluctant to continue. Implicit in such rugby player reactions is often the feeling that the bowling style is too tentative or "weak." In order to give all students an opportunity to appreciate the advantages of the bowling style, and to allow those who are natural bowlers to demonstrate their style with a minimum of inhibitions, it usually works best to start with "bowling."

Note: It may take several "takes" for this exercise to begin to work smoothly. However frustration, discomfort and impatience are part of the learning process and should be debriefed (see below).

Since natural bowlers may tend to be reluctant to give direct feedback, the instructor will need to do several things to create a classroom climate in which bowlers can give constructive, honest feedback to their rugby player partners:

A. First spend several sessions building a learning community through a variety of small group and paired activities in which observed bowlers are paired (one on one) with observed rugby players.

B. Throughout the course, actively elicit input from bowling style students, and demonstrate bowling type behaviors yourself as you listen, so bowlers don't get cut off by more assertive classmates. If the natural bowlers in the class feel that they can trust you and that you respect them and value their input, they are more likely to take the risk to give direct feedback to their partners when the time comes.

C. Demonstrate respect for, and understanding of, the advantages of bowling style interactions.

D. Rove and eavesdrop as partners are giving each other feedback. If you sense that a bowler is holding back and not telling his/her rugby style partner what he/she needs to hear, step in and quietly encourage the bowler by asking such questions as, "Did your partner perhaps interrupt a little too often?" or "Did your partner come across as a little too challenging and aggressive?"

5. In the same vein, if you sense that one of the rugby player's feedback to his/her bowler partner is too forceful and is overwhelming the bowler and causing loss of face, a hand on the arm of the rugby player, or some other calming non-verbal signal may help the rugby player rein themselves in a bit.

Some Suggested Discussion Topics: *(Topics should be pithy enough to engage all students in active conversation. If the conversation lags, introduce a new topic).*

The pros and cons of universalism and relativism (provide some prompts such as honor killings, female circumcision, political prisoners).

What does it mean to be "white" in America?

Does equality of opportunity really exist in the U.S.?

What changes could be made to improve this course? Which activities are worth keeping and which are not? What about assignments? Grading?

What type of a final exam do we think the instructor should give?

Are there ethnic enclaves in our community? What function do they serve? Have you ever walked through a neighborhood and felt you did not belong? What gave you that feeling? What did you do about it?

Debriefing: *After each Challenge (I, II, and III), debrief the students' experience by asking the following questions:*

1. *How many of you would label yourselves natural "bowlers"? This next question is just for you: How did it feel to participate in the bowling style conversation? How did it feel when your team switched to the rugby style conversation? (Call upon individual students as necessary).*

2. *How many of you would label yourselves natural "rugby players"? This next question is just for you: How did it feel to participate in the bowling style conversation? How did it feel when your team switched to the rugby style conversation? (Call upon individual students as necessary).*

Students may respond as follows...

Bowlers: On bowling style:
"It was easier to participate." "I had more time to think." "I like that I was not interrupted." "It felt more cooperative." "We got a lot of good ideas on the table."

Bowlers: On rugby style:
"It was really hard to demonstrate the target behaviors. I felt as if I were being very rude and aggressive." "I just listened." "I tend not to participate in this type of conversation." "The others talked really loudly." "There was no chance to get a word in edgewise." "I tried to make a point, but I got cut off." "I did what was expected, but it felt really awkward." "It was kind of fun, but tough."

Rugby Players: On bowling style:
"The conversation was really slow." "When I had to wait to speak, I sometimes forgot what I wanted to say!" "I felt as if I had been gagged and my hands had been tied behind my back!" "There was no energy." "It was boring." "I heard from some people I hadn't heard from before." "We generated some good ideas." "We took the activity more seriously."

Rugby Players: On rugby style:
"The conversation moved more quickly." "There was more energy." "We got a lot done." "I noticed that some people did not talk." "We argued a lot." "We didn't listen to each other very well."

Nonverbal
Communication
Activities

Nonverbal Observation Activity

Objective: To give students an understanding of nonverbal communication rules as well as assist them in appreciating the strong reactions we have to rules violations.

Preparation:
- Put students into groups of three.
- Have students number themselves 1, 2, and 3. This will help determine who is interacting and who is observing.
- Provide each student with two observation forms, one for each round they are observing, and explain the terms.

Task: During each 2–3 minute round, two students will interact and one will observe and record his or her observations on the form. Those interacting will engage in conversation (anything they'd like to discuss—the class, their weekend, their major, etc.). However, during this conversation, they will be asked to follow certain nonverbal communication rules. The round schedule follows.

Round One: Persons 1 and 2 engage in normal conversation.
              Person 3 observes.

Round Two: Persons 1 and 2 continue their conversation maintaining touch the entire time. (Whatever is comfortable—touching fingers, toes, holding hands, etc.)
              Person 3 observes.

Round Three: Persons 2 and 3 engage in conversation while maintaining constant eye contact.
              Person 1 observes.

Round Four: Persons 2 and 3 continue their conversation while avoiding eye contact.
              Person 1 observes.

Round Five: Persons 1 and 3 engage in conversation standing at least 5 feet apart.
              Person 2 observes.

Round Six: Persons 1 and 3 engage in conversation standing as closely as they can.
                (Note: "As closely as you can" is ambiguous enough to elicit different reactions from students. Instructing students to "freeze" at the end of the round and look around the room will provide interesting results.)
                Person 2 observes.

Debriefing: Give students some time to share their observations with each other. Then discuss their observations, perceptions, reactions, feelings, etc. as a class. Some discussion questions might be:

- Which was the most difficult round and why?
- Could you determine when people were uncomfortable? How?
- What changed the most on your observation form?
- Did you feel uncomfortable as an observer?
- How did you feel as a participant?
- Were there any factors, other than the nonverbal communication rules, that made you uncomfortable or more comfortable?
- Does everyone react the same way?
- Have you experienced any of these rules violations in real life?

Adapted from SFSU Speech Communication Graduate Studies, San Francisco, CA.

— Judgment Activities —

D.I.E.

The D.I.E. exercise (Wendt, 1984) helps students to understand how we process information. It is a useful tool in that it teaches students to pay attention to what causes their judgment, instead of going with their gut reaction. In addition, it teaches students to understand that there is more than one interpretation to any situation, and that their initial interpretation is not always correct. Paying closer attention to the description of one's behavior instead of the evaluation of that behavior helps students to understand that a behavior may be culturally bound.

D.I.E. is similar to perception checking, but its utility lies in that it can be done without clarification from the other person. Consequently, if someone is experiencing a critical incident and does not feel comfortable interacting with the other person, D.I.E. becomes a helpful strategy.

Description – This is where students should begin, describing the picture as objectively as possible, using factual statements.

Interpretations – Students should develop as many interpretations as possible. In other words, have students guess what is happening in the picture and determine the meaning.

Evaluation – The students' judgments of the situation are largely dependent on which interpretation they decide is the best one. (i.e., Is it OK? Not OK? Good? Bad? Scary? No big deal? etc.)

Students should spend time individually determining the description, interpretations, and evaluations using the form adjacent to the picture. This can be done as homework or in class. Once students have completed their individual determinations, class discussion can follow, recording a variety of descriptions, interpretations, and evaluations on a chalk board, flip chart, overhead projector, etc.

While using the picture is rather limited, it provides a classroom opportunity for students to try out the steps. Since the steps are more difficult than they seem, it is good practice for the students. The picture was created by the Anti-Defamation League and is intended to be ambiguous.

_____ Release Form _____

I hereby grant to Ellen Shide Crannell the absolute right and permission to reproduce the student activity I have prepared entitled _____ in the book entitled _Practicing Intercultural Communication_ and in future printings and editions. I further consent to the publication and copyrighting of this book to be published by Kendall/Hunt Publishing Company in any manner they may see fit. Proper acknowledgment of my work will be made at the author's discretion. This release form will in no way restrict republication of my material in any other form by me or others authorized by me.

Signature _____

Name _____

Address _____

City _____

State/Zip _____

Phone Number _____

Date _____